D1516182

# Strategic
# Policy Changes
# at
# Private Colleges

378.23
A549s EDU
LB
2341
.A596
1977

# Strategic Policy Changes at Private Colleges

## Educational and Fiscal Implications

Richard E. Anderson

Assisted by Jerry N. Haar

23477

Teachers College Press
Teachers College, Columbia University
New York and London

COVER BY FRANK MARSHALL

Copyright © 1977 by Teachers College, Columbia University.
All rights reserved.
Published by Teachers College Press, 1234 Amsterdam Avenue, New York,
NY 10027.

**Library of Congress Cataloging in Publication Data**

Anderson, Richard E    1943–
    Strategic policy changes at private colleges.

    Includes bibliographical references.
    1.   Universities and colleges–United States–Administration. 2.   Uni-
versities and  colleges–United  States–Finance. I.   Haar,  Jerry,  1947–
joint author. II.   Title.
LB2341.A596          378.73          77-13257
ISBN 0-8077-2543-9

Manufactured in the United States of America

# Contents

# List of Figures

# List of Tables

# Acknowledgments

Many people contributed to this book and I am indebted to them. Jerry Haar was an invaluable colleague and partner in the research. He suffered long hours and a frenetic travel schedule. Kassie Billingsly, Lynn McGowan, and Stu Varden assisted in data analysis. Hans Jenny offered excellent advice for the financial analysis. Len Baird and Jim Bess provided valuable consultation on the use and interpretation of CUES as well as general editorial assistance. Robert Parsonage and William Lovell assisted in the refinement of the religiosity index. Bob Pace graciously shared CUES data with us. Joel Meyerson was particularly helpful in the final editing.

Finally, all of the people at the Exxon Education Foundation deserve special thanks. Without their multifaceted support, the project and the book would not have been possible. An extra thanks goes to Dick Johnson, who was willing to listen to the ideas of a relatively young and inexperienced researcher.

All errors in fact or judgment are, of course, the author's.

# Foreword

As we contemplate the future of privately controlled colleges in the United States, we hear all around us warnings that institutional disappearance will be rampant and massive. At times the dismal forecasts dwell on the probable decline in the quality of the services, educational and otherwise, offered by these institutions. It is more and more fashionable to speculate that within another decade a large public sector of higher education and a much smaller than now privately controlled segment of elitist colleges and universities, few in number and rich enough to withstand the demographic vicissitudes of tomorrow, will have survived.

In the face of recent and the anticipation of future economic difficulties, a growing number of policy-makers and professionals have begun to ask themselves how one might distinguish a winning institution from a declining one in terms that stress more than the strictly financial variables. The present work by Richard E. Anderson contributes to this rapidly growing body of literature.

The author has chosen a difficult topic and answered the question before him in a manner that is both provocative and balanced. Without a doubt, his findings will be controversial if for no other reason than that there does not yet exist anything like a consensus on how one would or should respond to the question he poses.

Richard E. Anderson has taken to heart the admonition offered by the Commission on the Financing of Postsecondary Education—money is a means to an end, and financial inadequacy in higher educational institutions must be judged in terms of its effect on the scope and quality of their educational and related activities.

The author's findings in themselves are not all that surprising, and he reinforces much of what modern price theory has been saying about markets where product differentiation is in evidence. On the other hand, there is a message for planners: you purchase your economic improvement at a cost of which you should be aware. With a broadening of one's market appeal goes a loss of uniqueness, and this may portend trouble ahead.

Uniqueness in this instance is defined in terms of the colleges' religious missions and the sex composition of their student bodies.

Although this may not satisfy those who look for the strictly educational in a college, it allows the author to observe the sort of controlled before-and-after effects researchers seldom have an opportunity to study in quite the manner possible here. Policymakers may find interesting a discussion of institutional differentiation that encompasses the values Anderson investigates.

The reader will have to judge whether the evidence presented supports the conclusions and how well suited the policy recommendations are. One should note, however, that in the section on financial analysis, some concepts and information are offered that surprisingly are not yet standard elements in similar earlier analyses. Howard Bowen and John Minter are among the few others who recently have been pressing for this sort of information. Whether one likes it or not, the presence or absence of adequate monetary resources will determine whether a good college will become ill and a weak institution will gain educational strength. Knowledge of how expendable depreciated net assets have evolved over time can tell us much about an institution's future. It is to be wished that others will refine this type of analysis.

Until our national statistical agencies wake up to the need for functional financial and other relevant data designed to help policymakers analyze the health of higher educational institutions, researchers like Anderson will be severely limited in what they can tell us. At the same time, the author of this volume helps make a contribution to the future design of an appropriate statistical apparatus. We commend him and others who are interested in assessing the health of our colleges to forge ahead and build on the groundwork laid to date by those who have been devoting their time and skills to this important and timely subject. And we trust that policy-makers, legislators, and funders realize the need for adequate financial support so that the scientific discussion and the development of appropriate concepts and data can move ahead speedily while there still exists a broad viable private sector offering distinct and quality educational services.

Hans H. Jenny

*Rowsburg, Ohio*
*July 1977*

# Preface

As the task of maintaining enrollments becomes increasingly more difficult, many institutions of higher education are broadening their educational goals. Administrations at these colleges trust that a more "general" institutional mission will expand their college's applicant pool and, thereby, increase enrollment.

This study examines 40 private colleges that were single-sex and/or religious in the middle 1960's. Some have become coeducational; others have become more secular in their orientation; still others have changed very little with respect to these missions. By contrasting ten-year enrollment and fiscal trends for "change" and "non-change" institutions, evidence of the financial success of the changes to coeducation or more secular education was obtained. Moreover, all colleges in this study used the College and University Environmental Scales in the middle 1960's. By readministering this measure at each campus, a longitudinal assessment of environmental variation was added to the analysis. Additional perspective and depth was obtained through visits to each college and discussions with key administrators.

*Colleges that expanded their missions increased enrollments somewhat more rapidly than those that did not. Adverse environmental consequences appear to have accompanied these changes, however.* For example, at Roman Catholic colleges that became more secular, "sense of community" and "campus morale" fell dramatically. At female colleges that admitted men, the declines were even greater. At "non-change" Catholic and "non-change" female colleges, declines in these two measures were more modest. Moreover, colleges that did not alter their historic mission tended to improve on measures of academic orientation and student-faculty relationships. The "change" colleges did not.

It is more difficult to assess the environmental drift that followed secularization at colleges with a Protestant heritage because of problems with the sample. The evidence suggests, however, that the divergence that occurred between "change" and "non-change" Catholic colleges was paralleled by "change" and "non-change" Protestant colleges; with the divergence coming some years earlier.

*The financial analysis reveals that policy changes at the hitherto Catholic and female colleges were typically made under fiscal duress. Colleges that broadened their mission tended to be underenrolled and heavily in debt prior to adoption of change.* Although these policy changes brought more students, the fiscal improvement that occurred seems to have been achieved primarily by thrift—spreading financial resources more thinly and reducing instructional expenditures—rather than through increased tuition revenue.

On the basis of the evidence gathered for this study, *the change from single-sex to coeducation at male colleges seems to be uniformly successful*: enrollment increased more rapidly, SAT scores fell less rapidly, financial strain was less evident, and the educational environment, as measured by CUES, improved.

Although many colleges in the study possess an underlying financial strength, *an increasing number of colleges are experiencing cash flow difficulties*. To avoid the "snowball" effect that these problems can bring, *it recommended that private institutions be granted access to a "public line of credit."*

Most colleges in this study broadened their mission for financial rather than educational reasons. The decline in the number of single-sex and religious colleges is unfortunate because public institutions cannot assume these missions. *The real loss, however, is that the special and distinctive educational environments that characterize the special purpose college is rapidly disappearing.* Although the decline in the number of single-sex and religious colleges may be attributed to irreversible social trends, the truth remains that these colleges were not, and are not, competing on their educational merits alone. Many students who would and could profit from the educational environment of these colleges are dissuaded by their relatively high tuition charges. Until the extra cost of attending these institutions (versus public institutions) is reduced for the *middle-income* student, one can anticipate a further decline in the number of special purpose colleges.

## Chapter 1

# Introduction

Currently, officials at private colleges are confronted by a disturbing paradox. Elementary price theory (not to mention common sense) asserts that one cannot market a product at a higher price than the competition unless the product is distinct and serves a special need.[1] The higher the price differential, the greater the distinctiveness (marginal utility) must be. The extra cost of attending a private four-year college, vis-à-vis a comparable public four-year institution, can exceed three thousand dollars. In light of this price discrepancy, the successful private college must certainly be distinctive—that is, different, although not necessarily elitist. Paradoxically, the more distinctive the college, the smaller the potential student market and the more difficult it is to maintain enrollments.

In spite of the obvious need of private colleges to be "special," administrators at many private colleges are broadening the missions of their institutions with the expectation of expanding the potential applicant pool and, thereby, increasing enrollment. Selective colleges are admitting underprepared students. Liberal arts colleges are adding a "career orientation." Two-year colleges are adding four-year degrees. Four-year colleges are adding two-year and graduate degrees. Religiously-oriented colleges are becoming more secular, and single-sex colleges are becoming coeducational. The present study has selected the last two of these changes for review. This selection was made because, of all the dimensions of competition for students, there are only two from which public colleges are legally excluded—religious and single-sex education.[2] If private colleges do not provide these types of higher education, they will not be available. Yet in spite of this legal prerogative, the number of private single-sex colleges declined from 515 in the Autumn of 1965 to 156 in the Autumn of 1973.[3] During this same period, the number of institutions claiming religious affiliation declined from 910 to 790.[4] Moreover, this latter change does not include those colleges that have become more secular but still declare church affiliation.

One is tempted to attribute the changes toward more secular education and coeducation to societal changes. Undoubtedly changing values are part of the reason. The fact remains, however, that the tuition gap between public institutions and these special-purpose private colleges is several thousand dollars a year and growing. Students who would prefer, with all else being equal, a special-purpose college are finding the cost increasingly unequal. As this occurs, more students and their families will chose a college for economic, rather than educational, reasons.[5]

Religious, male, and female colleges, by virtue of their church ties or single-sex admissions policies, contribute significantly to the diversity of American higher education. If these colleges have a unique educational environment that is lost as they broaden their mission, this loss is indeed unfortunate. Public officials must consider this issue as they set policies that affect these independent institutions of higher education.

In addition to the issue facing public officials, there are also questions about the effectiveness of a broadened mission. If single-sex colleges become coeducational, will the applicant pool increase? Will these changes ease financial stress? Are there alternatives? What are the educational/cultural implications? What are the longer-range competitive implications?

This report summarizes a study of 40 private colleges that were either religiously-oriented or single-sex in the middle 1960's. Some of these colleges significantly broadened their missions, some did not. By comparing ten-year environmental and financial trends, this report provides evidence for administrators faced with the strategic questions noted above. The findings also have significance for public officials, with regard to the issue of maintaining diversity in American higher education.

There is little doubt that these matters are critical. As Howard Bowen and John Minter phrased the question in their recent report on private higher education:

> One major question . . . [is] whether, in the struggle for survival, the basic integrity of private colleges and universities is threatened. With the growing intensity of competition for students and funds, are they being forces to respond to market forces in ways that impair their distinctiveness, their academic excellence, their concern for human scale and individual personality, their commitment to liberal learning, their role as a sanctuary of academic freedom, their position as stan-dard-setters? It would be a hollow victory if the private sector were to survive and even prosper financially at the expense of giving up the characteristics that make their survival important.[6]

## Chapter 2

# Methodology

## The Sample

In the planning stages of this study, it became apparent that the most difficult aspect would be evaluating environmental trends. To make this assessment, the College and University Environment Scales (CUES) were employed. 175 single-sex or religiously oriented colleges were identified as having administered CUES in the 1960's. All were considered for inclusion in this study. A brief questionnaire was mailed to each institution to obtain more detailed information. Of the 103 that responded, 48 colleges were invited to participate in the study. They were selected so that Protestant, Catholic, male, and female colleges would all be represented. In addition, the following criteria, listed in order of priority, were used for selection:

1. The clearest and most extreme examples of religious, single-sex, and change colleges were chosen.
2. Data on other institutional changes were collected. Institutions that were most stable in other ways were given priority in the selection procedure.
3. When possible, colleges taking CUES earlier in the 1960's were selected.
4. Large universities were avoided because of their complexity.

Of the 48 colleges invited, 40 agreed to join the study and formed the final sample. Henceforth, they are referred to as the *study colleges*.

Final Categorization

As more detailed information was gathered on the 40 study colleges, the initial classification was refined further.

The task was fairly straightforward vis-à-vis single-sex colleges. If 90% or more of a student body was of one sex, the college was considered single-sex. Thus "change" institutions were those that were over 90% single-sex when CUES was first administered but less than 90% in 1975-76. Although it would have been possible for a college with 10% men in 1965 and 11% men in 1975-76 to be labeled "female-change," in practice this did not occur. More commonly, a "change" college would have a very few students of the opposite sex in 1965 (two or three) and a large number in 1975-76 (25% of the student body). Unfortunately, only one college in the sample admitted just men in 1975-76. The category of single-sex male was therefore excluded from the analysis.

The task of differentiating "religious-change" from "religious" institutions proved more difficult. The scale of church/college relationships developed by Patillo and Mackenzie[1] was particularly useful in this effort. Using many of Patillo's and Mackenzie's measures, potential index components were selected to facilitate a retroactive assessment and consistent evaluation of the religious environment at each institution. These components must be considered as proxies; however, it would have been preferable to have used a more direct assessment—perhaps to have compared student's responses longitudinally using identical questions about the religious environment—but this was not feasible. Consequently, the researchers relied on institutional-type indicators of religious orientation. Henceforth this will be referred to as the *religiosity index*.

The religiosity index uses eight items to create a composite score:

1.  Percentage of full-time equivalent (FTE) students of the same denomination as the college. (At institutions where the percentage was above the median for their denomination in the reference year, one point was added.)
2.  Percentage of total church support: church donations *and* contributed services. (At institutions where the percentage

was above the median for their denomination in the reference year, one point was added.)

3.  Religious requirements for membership on the governing board. (If a majority of governing board members must be church members, one point was added.)

4.  Required chapel attendance. (One point.)

5.  Compulsory religion courses. (One point.)

6.  Moral demands. (These may entail the specific prohibition, due either to articles of faith by a sect or to custom, of activities that are commonplace at the vast majority of American colleges; or they may be positive in nature, such as the requirement of human service internships. (One point.)

7.  Statement of purpose: religion. (If the statement of purpose in the catalog specifically mentioned religion, one point was added.)

8.  Statement of purpose: denomination. (If the statement of purpose in the catalog specifically mentioned denomination, one point was added.)

Institutional composite scores ranged from a low of 0 to a high of 8. For each institution identified as church-related during the reference year, a composite score was calculated and listed. The same was done for these colleges for the 1975-76 academic year. Colleges that scored 3 or greater in the reference year but less than 3 in the 1975-76 year were considered "change" institutions; those that had index scores of 3 or greater in both the reference year and the 1975-76 year were classified as "non-change" institutions.

Sample Definitions

Terms used to identify sub-groups in the sample are defined below:

*Study colleges*: all 40 colleges in the study.

*Protestant colleges*: colleges with a Protestant heritage that scored higher than 3 on the index in both the reference and 1975-76 years.

*Protestant-change colleges*: colleges with a Protestant heritage that scored higher than 3 on the index in the reference year but less than 3 in 1975-76.

*Protestant-heritage colleges*: both Protestant and Protestant-change colleges.

*Catholic colleges*: colleges with a Roman Catholic heritage that scored higher than 3 on the index in both the reference year and 1975-76.

*Catholic-change colleges*: colleges with a Roman Catholic heritage that scored higher than 3 on the index in the reference year but less than 3 in 1975-76.

*Catholic-heritage colleges*: both Catholic and Catholic-change colleges.

*Female colleges*: colleges that indicated that 90% or more of their student body was female in September of the reference year and in September of 1975-76.

*Female-change colleges*: colleges that indicated that 90% or more of their student body was female in September of the reference-year but less than 90% was female in September of 1975-76.

*Male-change colleges*: colleges that indicated that 90% or more of their student body was male in September of the reference-year but less than 90% was male in September of 1975-76.

*Reference year*: the academic year in which a college had first taken CUES.

*Current year* (for the study): 1975-76

Discussion of Sample

As this index was created and as the colleges were visited, it became apparent that there was a marked difference between Protestant and Roman Catholic institutions vis-à-vis religiosity. A brief discussion of these differences is included here because of their importance in interpreting the results.

In the reference year, the Protestant-heritage colleges were biomodally distributed on the index; the two modes were 7 and 4. Moreover, the reference-year index score was highly predictive of the current-year index score. The average reference-year score for Protestant colleges was 7.3, for Protestant-change colleges it was 4.9 (see Table 1). From discussions with campus officials, it became clear that the colleges labeled Protestant-change had already begun

## Table 1

### AVERAGE RELIGIOSITY INDEX SCORES

|  | N | Average Index Score | |
| --- | --- | --- | --- |
|  |  | Reference Year | 1975-1976 |
| Protestant colleges | 7 | 7.3 | 6.6 |
| Protestant-change colleges | 6 | 4.9 | 1.7 |
| Catholic colleges | 12 | 5.4 | 3.6 |
| Catholic-change colleges | 11 | 4.6 | 1.5 |

to secularize (as this process is operationally defined for this study) *before* the reference year. For example, administrators at Protestant-change colleges would typically refer back to the 1950's and early 1960's when discussing the religious changes at their colleges. Thus, conclusions from these data about the impact of secularization at these two groups of institutions are restricted.

Catholic colleges were much more uniformly distributed on the index in the reference year. The mode was 5, and the difference between the averages for the two groups was slight. By 1975-76, *all* the Catholic and Catholic-change colleges had declined on the index. In discussions with college officials, the major reason cited was the far-reaching effects of the Second Vatican Council, which was concluded in the middle 1960's. Greely, McCready, and McCourt have also noted the importance of socio-economic changes among American Catholic and the encyclical letter *Humanae Vitae* as factors affecting (and afflicting) Catholic schools in this country.[2] Regardless of exact causes, colleges with a Catholic heritage show a more uniform decline on the index. Although this trend was confirmed by discussions with campus officers, the index did appear to discriminate accurately among Roman Catholic colleges on the degree of secularization.

Table 2 is a categorization of the study colleges. As noted, there was only one male college that did not become coeducational,

Table 2

## DISTRIBUTIONS OF THE STUDY COLLEGES BY RELIGIOUS ORIENTATION AND SEX COMPOSITION OF THE STUDENT BODY

|  | Protestant | Protestant-Change | Catholic | Catholic-Change | Secular | Total by Sex |
|---|---|---|---|---|---|---|
| Female | 0 | 0 | 9 | 1 | 3 | 13 |
| Female-change | 0 | 0 | 0 | 5 | 0 | 5 |
| Male | 0 | 1 | 0 | 0 | 0 | 1 |
| Male-change | 0 | 1 | 2 | 2 | 1 | 6 |
| Coeducational | 7 | 4 | 1 | 3 | 0 | 15 |
| Total by Religion | 7 | 6 | 12 | 11 | 4 | 40 |

and therefore no analysis was done for this category. Another problem is that all five female-change colleges were also Catholic-change colleges; the analysis of female-change colleges must be understood within that context. This does not imply, however, that other types of female colleges that became coeducational would exhibit financial and educational conditions markedly dissimilar from these colleges. Moreover, by contrasting female-change with Catholic-change colleges, one can make an indirect determination of the separate impact of coeducation.

Table 3 presents the geographical distribution of the study colleges. Except for the lack of colleges from the Far West, the study colleges tend to represent the distribution of all small private colleges.

## Measuring the Environment

This study employed the College and University Environment Scales (CUES), which was developed by C. Robert Pace and is distributed by the Educational Testing Service (E.T.S.). Each of the 40 study colleges had administered CUES in the 1960's—most in

Table 3

GEOGRAPHICAL DISTRIBUTION OF STUDY COLLEGES

|  | N | % |
|---|---|---|
| New England | 4 | 10.0 |
| Middle Atlantic | 12 | 30.0 |
| Southeast | 9 | 22.5 |
| Great Lakes | 6 | 15.0 |
| Plains | 8 | 20.0 |
| Southwest | 1 | 2.5 |

the middle of the decade (see Table 4). By comparing the 1975-76 results with those obtained earlier, an assessment of environment change was obtained.[3]

CUES

CUES employs the responses of students to 100 true/false items[4] to measure the campus environment on seven dimensions: Scholarship, Awareness, Community, Propriety, Practicality, Campus Morale, and Quality of Teaching and Student-Faculty Relationships. In addition, the second version allows the test administrator to include ten "Local Option" questions. Most study colleges distributed Local Option questions supplied by the researcher. When appropriate, these results are used to supplement other findings.

To score the scales, one point is added to the base score[5] for each item of the scale that has been answered in the "keyed direction" by more than 66% of the respondents; one point is subtracted for each item that is answered in the "keyed direction" by fewer than 33%. The keyed directions may be either true or false. The *CUES: Second Edition Technical Manual* defines the seven scales as follows.

Scale 1. Practicality: The 20 items that contribute to the score for this scale describe an environment characterized by enterprise, organization, material benefits,

## Table 4

### DISTRIBUTION OF STUDY COLLEGES BY DATE OF ORIGINAL CUES[a]

|  | N | % | Cumulative % |
|---|---|---|---|
| 1964-65 | 9 | 22.5 | 22.5 |
| 1965-66 | 13 | 32.5 | 55.0 |
| 1966-67 | 5 | 12.5 | 67.5 |
| 1967-68 | 4 | 10.0 | 77.5 |
| 1968-69 | 6 | 15.0 | 92.5 |
| 1969-70 | 3 | 7.5 | 100.0 |

[a]Time lapse to second CUES administration:
  Median = 10 years
  Mode = 10 years
  Mean = 9 years

and social activities. There are both vocational and collegiate emphases. A kind of orderly supervision is evident in the administration and the classwork. As in many organized societies there is also some personal benefit and prestige to be obtained by operating in the system— knowing the right people, being in the right clubs, becoming a leader, respecting one's superiors, and so forth. The environment, though structured, is not repressive; it responds to entrepreneurial activities and is generally characterized by good fun and school spirit.

Scale 2. Community: The items in this scale describe a friendly, cohesive, group-oriented campus. There is a feeling of group welfare and group loyalty that encompasses the college as a whole. The atmosphere is cogenial; the campus is a community. Faculty members know the students, are interested in their problems, and go out of their way to be helpful. Student life is characterized by togetherness and sharing rather than by privacy and cool detachment.

Scale 3. Awareness: This scale reflects a concern about, and emphasis upon, three sorts of meaning—personal, poetic, and political. An emphasis upon self-understanding, reflectiveness, and identity suggests the search for personal meaning. A wide range of opportunities for creative and appreciative relationships to painting, music, drama, poetry, sculpture, architecture, and the like suggests the search for poetic meaning. A concern about events around the world, the welfare of mankind, and the present and future conditions of man suggests the search for political meaning and idealistic commitment. What seems to be evident in this sort of environment is a stress on awareness—an awareness of self, of society, and of aesthetic stimuli. Along with this push toward expansion, and perhaps as a necessary condition for it, there is an encouragement of questioning and dissent and a tolerance of nonconformity and personal expressiveness.

Scale 4. Propriety: These items describe an environment that is polite and considerate. Caution and thoughtfulness are evident. Group standards of decorum are important. There is an absence of demonstrative, assertive, argumentative, risk-taking activities. In general the campus atmosphere is mannerly, considerate, proper, and conventional.

Scale 5. Scholarship: The items in this scale describe a campus characterized by intellectuality and scholastic discipline. The emphasis is on competitively high academic achievement and a serious interest in scholarship. The pursuit of knowledge and theories, scientific or philosophical, is carried on rigorously and vigorously. Intellectual speculation, an interest in ideas, knowledge for its own sake, and intellectual discipline—all these are characteristic of the environment.

Scale 6. Campus Morale: The 22 items in this scale indicate acceptance of social norms, group cohesiveness, friendly assimilation into campus life, and, at the same time, a commitment to intellectual pursuits and freedom of expression. Intellectual goals are exemplified and widely shared in an atmosphere of personal and social relationships that are both supportive and spirited.

Scale 7. Quality of Teaching and Faculty-student Relationships: This 11-item scale defines an atmosphere in which professors are perceived to be scholarly, to set high standards, to be clear, adaptive, and flexible. At the same time, this academic quality of teaching is infused with warmth, interest, and helpfulness toward students.[6]

Although the dimensions are relevant to the colleges under study, their precision may be questioned. The *Technical Manual* provides a detailed discussion of the reliability and validity of the instruments. On the subject of reliability, Pace concludes:

From this empirical evidence it seems reasonable to say that, in general, a given score is probably quite stable within a margin of 3 points. The chances are 4 out of 5 that with a comparable sample, the obtained score will not differ by more than 3 points; and the chances are 3 out of 5 that it will not differ by more than 2 points.[7]

Validity is a more problematic and, to some extent, semantic issue. Pace reviews a number of other institutional indicators, such as number of students, percentage of faculty with doctorates, and library holdings. He also correlates the scores on his scales with indices used by others. In summary, he finds:

The overall network of correlations between CUES scores and other data can be characterized as broadly supportive of associations one might reasonably expect. The conclusion from such associations is that campus atmosphere, as measured by CUES is a concept buttressed by a good deal of concurrent validity.[8]

Although there can be no definitive answer to the validity question (e.g., to a great extent a scholarly campus depends upon what one values as scholarly), this study accepts these measures as evidence. Reservations about the measures are discussed in the analysis of the results. These reservations notwithstanding, the author believes that the data collected in this study provide the best available evidence on the ten-year environmental trends at these colleges.

## Reporting the Results

The results are reported in three ways: median scale scores, item response, and a Summary Estimate of Distinctiveness.

The primary method of presentation is to chart the seven median scale scores for each group of colleges. Each of the median scores is scaled against 1965-66 normative data reported in the *Technical Manual*.

To add further detail and clarification, the response rates to selected items are reviewed and included when appropriate. For example, there are 20 items in the scholarship scale. At female colleges, item number 62, asking whether "most courses are a real intellectual challenge," showed the greatest change in response rate. 45% of all students at these single-sex colleges indicated that this was true in the 1960's; 69% agreed in 1975-76.

Finally, a Summary Estimate of Distinctiveness (SED) is created. This measure is a normalized sum of squared deviations; its purpose is to provide a summary measure of deviation from the norms. The SED is calculated as follows:

$$ \text{SED} = \sum_{i=1}^{7} \left( \frac{\overline{X}_{ij} - \overline{Y}_i}{\sigma_i} \right)^2, $$

where

$\overline{X}_{ij}$ = mean score on scale i for the colleges in sub-group j

$\overline{Y}_i$ = mean score on scale i for the 100 colleges used to establish norms

$\sigma_i$ = standard deviation for all 100 colleges on scale i

i = seven scales

j = sub-group

Lest the research be accused of pretentious empiricism, a number of qualifications are recognized. For example, peaks and valleys affect this statistic equally. Also, changes at the outer reaches of the scales have more impact than changes close to the norm. The SED is used only as a convenient quantitative summary measure. It is, of course, meant to be used cautiously.

## Financial/Operating Assessment

In many respects, this study incorporates and expands the research of others. Collier and Carroll have proposed ratio measures; the author of this report is in debt to them for providing their draft material.[9] Bowen and Minter have used ratio measures and have also made corrections for price changes in their recent publications.[10] Anderson and Lanier adjust their data for price changes,[11] using the new Higher Education Price Indexes (HEPI) developed by Halstead.[12]

This report relies heavily on Halstead's work and supplements his data with the price indices developed for liberal arts colleges by Wynn.[13] Another principle of this report has been the combination, when possible, of fund data. Critics have urged colleges to consolidate their fund accounting reports; among them are Jenny of the College of Wooster,[14] Bastable of Columbia University's Graduate School of Business,[15] Price, Waterhouse, and Company,[16] and Wilkinson of the University of Rochester.[17] Further, this study draws directly from the techniques used for security analysis.[18]

Following is an annotated review of the principles used for financial measurement in this study.

## Consolidated Balance Sheet

College and university financial reporting practices have historically focused on the control and use of funds accrued from separate sources. From this principle of stewardship has evolved college and university fund accounting—separately aggregating and reporting financial information. Although one is reluctant to quarrel with the need to maintain separate record for certain funds, it is difficult to reconcile the extremes to which this principle is carried—that is, the absence of a final aggregation in the financial reports. Colleges and universities, of course, are not in the business of maximizing return on total equity or on total assests. But they are presumably attempting to maximize educational return on the college's assets or equity. The trends of assets and equity are there- fore important. As mentioned, there have been critics of conven- tional reporting practices. To cite a more specific example, two accounting professors at Cornell University have reported that ten major eastern universities reported deficits totaling 3.6 million dollars in 1969-70; total equity at these institutions increased 990 million dollars in the same year.[19] Although the consolidation of fund data would not fully resolve their inherent criticism, it does provide financial reviewers with more comprehensive information.

In this study, balance sheet, and only balance sheet, informa- tion was aggregated. A list of the definitions and procedures fol- lows:

1. The agency fund was excluded from the analysis.
2. Assets were subdivided into three categories: (a) liquid assets, (b) other assets, and (c) fixed assets. Liquid assets were considered to be all assets which could be readily converted into cash to meet current obligations. These assets include cash, stocks, bonds, and interest receivable. Cash in the loan fund was not considered liquid because this money is typically federal money or money matching federal funds. Fixed assets included all building, land, equipment, and construction in progress. The remaining assets were placed in the "other" category: accounts re- ceivable, inventories, student loan fund assets, and real estate holdings.
3. Liabilities were grouped in a fashion similar to assets: (a) short-term debt; (b) other debt, and (c) long-term debt. All obligations of the college requiring cash payment within one year (including interest payable, accrued wages, withheld taxes, and principal payments due) were put in the short-term debt grouping. Long-term debts are those liabilities of the colleges that are payable after one year (e.g., mortages and bonds). Debts not considered short- or long-term were grouped in the "other" category

and include deferred revenues, debts to religious orders that operate the institutions, and the federal portion of the NDSL loan funds.

4. Total equity (or net worth) is defined as the total of all funds, except agency. The separate fund balances were also examined.

5. Dealing with the loan fund presented a particular problem. Generally about eight-ninths of the loan fund is federal money. It was decided to include loan fund assets and count the federal portion of the funds as an "other" liability.

6. Inter-fund borrowings were eliminated except as they involved the agency fund.

## Combining Current Fund Unrestricted and Restricted Dollars

At many institutions, particularly research universities, an analysis that combined restricted and unrestricted current fund dollars would be likely to yield a meaningless aggregation.[20] For these small colleges, however, the simplicity gained by combining the two categories seemed worth the slight distortion. First, at the 21 colleges for which data were available, restricted income represented less than 10% of the total current fund income in 1975. Second, the restricted income at these colleges typically was closely related to their educational mission (e.g., student aid). If these restricted funds were unavailable, it is likely that they would need to be replaced with unrestricted money. Moreover, most of the colleges in 1965 and a sizable minority in 1975 did not report restricted income separately.

## Price Adjustments

To adjust the data so that they were comparable from one year to the next, the Higher Education Price Indexes (HEPI) were used. The more specialized set of indices of Wynn, created specifically for liberal arts colleges and subdivided by current fund categories, offers obvious advantages. Although these indices have not been kept current, they were used to make special corrections on instructional expenses. Price adjustments were applied only to operating income and expense data.[21]

## Per Student Adjustments

Another adjustment to establish comparability is to divide by units of output—in this case output is approximated by the number of full-time-equivalent students. This adjustment is made for both income and expense reports, as well as for the balance sheets.

## Specific Measures

This study concentrated its financial/operating analysis on five areas: (1) demand, (2) liquidity, (3) debt structure, (4) financial resources, and (5) operating results. In each area several measures were used; these are summarized in Table 5.

*Demand* for places is obviously of critical concern for these tuition-dependent institutions. A number of measures were used and the interrelationships among the measures are considered and discussed: enrollment, applications, percent accepted, percent of accepted students enrolling, percent of students receiving financial aid, average SAT scores, percent of commuting students, percent from out of state, and percent of the student body over the age of 25.

*Liquidity* measures are intended to probe the solvency of an institution; that is, how vulnerable the institution is to the demands of creditors. Specifically, the measures compare available resources with pressing debts. Fund data are clustered because an institution is unlikely to allow bankruptcy if it has sufficiently large "available" resources in any of its funds. These funds need to be "expendable," but even if they are restricted in some way, the money can be borrowed or used as collateral. The most direct measure is the ratio of liquid assets to short-term debt. For the purposes of this report, this ratio is called the *liquid ratio*. If it were considered analogous to the "current ratio" used by business, a measure of 2.0 might be considered adequate. But because inventories and accounts receivable were eliminated, we may wish to compare it with the "quick ratio," for which a value of 1.0 is often considered safe. Since inventories and receivables are so small, however, this standard might be too liberal. The preference of the researcher is not to norm such statistics on the ratios used by commercial enterprises but to look for normative data from similar institutions. A second measure is similar to the liquid ratio except endowment funds are exluded. Thus, it assesses the ability of the college to meet cash flow without tapping endowment. An additional reason for excluding endowment funds is that they are reported at "book value," which may be particularly misleading with respect to trend data. The final measure is *short-term debt as percent of current fund income*. This statistic scales short-term borrowing against dollar volume of operation.

*Debt Structure* statistics are intended to array the financial structure of the college. Are the colleges relying more upon debt? The most direct measure is the ratio of debt to equity. A second measure is total debt as a percent of current fund income. Again, this statistic scales debt against the volume of operation. The final measure selected is principal and interest payments as a percent of current fund income, or *debt burden*; this statistic estimates the relative drain of debt payments on the current fund.

The intent of *resources* criteria is to probe trends in the financial ability of the institution to deliver education. These measures are truly rudimentary proxies. Yet, all things being equal, a wealthy institution is more likely to succeed in its mission than is a poor one. The primary measure of resources is *total equity* or net worth —defined as the sum of all fund balances except the agency fund. The second measure, *equity per student*, corrects for the degree to which the equity must be spread. Finally, equity is adjusted by deducting estimates for depreciation.

*Operating Results* statistics rely heavily on the current fund income and expense statements, and detail revenue and expenditure patterns and associated statistics for the ten-year period. They are not individually reviewed here because they are commonly found in financial analyses of colleges and universities. The definition of surplus or deficit should be clarified, however. For this report, it is current fund income less both current fund expenditures and mandatory transfers.

## Collecting Financial Data

Each college was requested to submit audited financial statements for 1964-65, 1967-68, 1971-72, and 1974-75. Because of a

# Table 5

## MEASURES USED IN FINANCIAL/OPERATING ANALYSIS

| Demand | Liquidity | Debt Structures | Financial Resources | Operating Results |
|---|---|---|---|---|
| Enrollment | Liquid ratio | Debt/ equity ratio | Equity | Sources of income |
| Applications | Liquid ratio with endowment funds excluded | Total debt as a percent of current fund income | Equity per student | Relative expenditures |
| Percent accepted | Short-term debt as a percent of current fund income | Debt burden | | Student-faculty ratio |
| Percent enrolling | | | Equity with an estimate for depreciation deducted | Expenditures per student adjusted for price increases |
| Percent receiving financial aid | | | | Maintenance expenditures/ plant |
| Average SAT scores | | | | Student aid/ tuition |
| Percent commuting | | | | Surplus (deficit)/ student |
| Percent out-of-state | | | | |
| Percent over age 25 | | | | |

shift in data collection procedures after the project was initiated, occasionally the report of an adjacent year had to be substituted (e.g., 1968-69 for 1967-68). If a middle year was missing, linear extropolation was used to fill in the data gap. To validate the collected data, the estimates, and the measures developed, the chief business officers were questioned during the college visits. After reviewing the work sheets and findings with these officers, it became clear that what error remained in the statistics was not unduly troublesome. With minor exceptions, the indicators seemed to highlight well the ten-year fiscal trends. Occasionally new information would surface (e.g., an undetected accounting change) and the data were altered accordingly. In most instances, however, the business officers felt the measures were accurate and revealing.

### Survey

In addition to the environmental and financial analyses, key administrators (typically the president, chief academic officer, chief financial officer, and a trustee) were interviewed and given questionnaires.

The interviews and questionnaires covered a range of issues. For example: How have the goals and/or the policies changed in the past ten years? What were the internal and external forces of change? How were the decisions to change made, or did they simply evolve? How were the changes implemented? What were the anticipated and unanticipated effects of these changes on the college, generally? On the faculty? On the students? On the administration? How might things have been done differently? What future changes are being considered?

Obviously, it would have been impossible to gather complete information on all the areas identified above. This was not the intent. Rather, the researchers sought to understand the official's perception of the institutional environment and priorities, and to detect subtle (or not so subtle) attitudes, opinions, and feelings about issues, problems, and prospects that the research team determined to be relevant.

## Chapter 3

# Environmental Trends

> ... the typical small college is characterized by a more
> friendly atmosphere, closer contacts between faculty
> and students, a stronger identification with the institu-
> tion, and a feeling on the part of the students that they
> matter as individuals. ... these attributes are ... [likely
> to be] more conducive to student development than are
> the depersonalizing and alienating attributes of large in-
> stitutions.[1]

## All Study Colleges

The colleges in this study possess characteristics very similar
to those described above by Astin and Lee. The dotted line on
Figure 1 connects the 1960's median scale scores for all study colleges. The median Scholarship and Awareness scores were slightly
below the norm, the Practicality score, slightly above. On what
might be termed the personal aspects of the campus environment
(Community, Campus Morale, and Quality of Teaching), however,
the median scores for this group were quite high. These colleges
could be characterized as cohesive, friendly, and group-oriented.
Although the campus could not have been considered as particularly scholastic or intellectual, there was a supportive educational
environment and an acceptance of group norms. Moreover, the
quality of teaching and faculty-student relationships also appeared
to have been quite supportive. The most distinctive characteristic
of these colleges, according to this evidence, was a clear sense of
decorum. The typical campus was polite, proper, and mannerly.

## Figure 1

## CUES SUMMARY PROFILES: ALL COLLEGES

Number of students (1960's) = 4245
Number of students (1975-6) = 3205
Number of institutions = 40

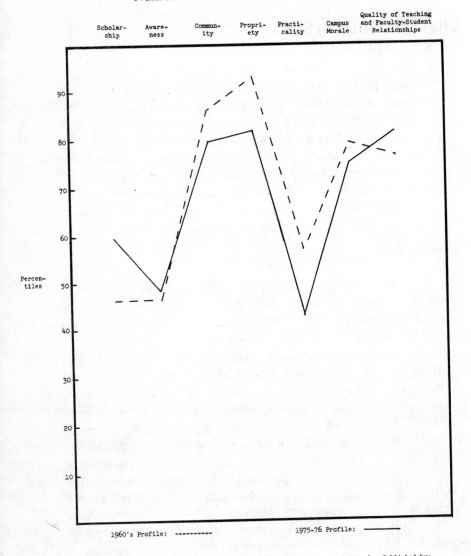

1960's Profile: ----------     1975-76 Profile: ————

This profile format is adapted from the CUES, Second Edition Technical Manual. Published by: Institutional Research Program for Higher Education, Educational Testing Service, Princeton, N.J.

By 1975-76, the general shape of the profile—for these institutions—had changed only slightly. The median scores for Scholarship and Quality of Teaching had risen, whereas those for Community, Campus Morale, and Practicality had declined. It would seem therefore, that these colleges had become somewhat more academic in their orientation, had retained or perhaps increased their emphasis on teaching, while losing some of the special personal and cohesive qualities that once characterized them. Finally, they declined ten percentile points in Propriety—indicating a less decorous and polite environment.

When interpreting these data, one should remember that the norm was established in 1965-66. It is possible that the responses at *all* colleges have shifted. If this is true, then the changes indicated with respect to the national norm may be exaggerated. Also, these responses reflect student perceptions and are only presumed to be grounded in reality. For example, the five items on the Scholarship scale that changed the most are give in Table 6. For each item, there are three interpretations. There may have been a real increase in academic standards set by professors and students. Or, these responses may evince a decline in student abilities. Thus, the same standards may loom as higher hurdles. A third explanation is that there may have been a drop in student expectations and standards; that is, the students are just as capable but they do not *expect* to be "pushed" or do not expect other students to take course work "seriously." There is no answer to the quandary. And so, with lack of better evidence, these data are presumed to be well grounded.[2]

The Awareness scale is intended to measure personal, poetic, and political concerns. Although the aggregate score changed very little, the item analysis yields an interesting, if not unexpected, finding. The responses to the five items that changed most are given in Table 7.

The three items for which responses increased in the keyed direction probe personal and poetic concerns, whereas the two questions that declined concern political awareness. Thus, reports about a rise in student introspection with a corresponding decline in political concerns are supported by this evidence.

An idea that helped shape this study was that private colleges must be different and distinctive if they are to compete effectively.

## Table 6

## VOLATILE ITEMS ON THE SCHOLARSHIP SCALE

| Item No. | Item | Keyed Direction | 1960's Percent | 1975-76 Percent | Change[a] |
|---|---|---|---|---|---|
| 62 | Most courses are a real intellectual challenge | True | 45.4 | 63.7 | +18.4 |
| 11 | Professors really push students | True | 30.9 | 45.2 | +14.4 |
| 61 | Most professors are thorough teachers and really probe fundamentals | True | 69.4 | 82.6 | +13.2 |
| 14 | Students set high standards of achievement for themselves | True | 52.1 | 64.0 | +11.9 |
| 70 | Students are very serious and purposeful about their work | True | 58.1 | 67.0 | +8.8 |

[a]In percentage points.

Although the profiles are an effective measure of uniqueness, they do not lend themselves to summary or comparison. The measure chosen to summarize quantitatively and to compare distinctiveness is the Summary Estimate of Distinctiveness (SED), described in the preceding chapter. The results are summarized in Table 8. The SED for all study colleges declined from 3.377 to 2.240. Although the author counsels against taking these statistics too literally, the results are graphically presented in Figure 1. The dotted line, representing the 1960's profile of median scores, is noticeably farther from the center than is the solid 1975-76 profile of medians. In sum, there is evidence of a general decline in distinctiveness.

Table 7

## VOLATILE ITEMS ON THE AWARENESS SCALE

| Item No. | Item | Keyed Direction | 1960's Percent | 1975-76 Percent | Change[a] |
|---|---|---|---|---|---|
| 81 | Students are encouraged to criticize policies and programs | True | 37.5 | 54.1 | +16.6 |
| 40 | Concerts and art exhibits draw big crowds of students | True | 26.5 | 40.3 | +13.8 |
| 39 | There is a lot of interest in poetry, music, painting, etc. | True | 41.5 | 55.1 | +13.6 |
| 33 | Students are actively concerned about international affairs | True | 54.7 | 37.7 | -17.0 |
| 37 | Controversial speakers stir a lot of student discussion | True | 73.4 | 55.7 | -17.7 |

[a]In percentage points.

## Results Grouped by the Religious Orientation of the Colleges

Protestant Colleges

Examining the results for Protestant colleges shown in Figure 2, one observes that the shape of the Protestant college profile in the 1960's resembles the profile of all study colleges at that time (although slightly higher in each category). By 1975-76, the median scores on each scale had declined. The declines were insignificant, however, except for the drop on the Practicality scale. To sum-

MICHIGAN CHRISTIAN COLLEGE LIBRARY
ROCHESTER, MICHIGAN

Table 8

SUMMARY ESTIMATE OF DISTINCTIVENESS (SED)

|  | SED 1960's | 1975-76 | Percent Difference |
|---|---|---|---|
| All colleges | 3.377 | 2.240 | -34 |
| Female | 6.228 | 4.872 | -22 |
| Female-change | 6.447 | 1.710 | -73 |
| Male-change | 0.801 | 1.178 | +47 |
| Protestant | 8.570 | 5.364 | -37 |
| Protestant-change | 2.158 | 1.929 | -11 |
| Catholic | 5.167 | 3.186 | -38 |
| Catholic-change | 2.473 | 1.161 | -53 |

marize, the general profile for Protestant colleges remained essentially unchanged over the time period of the study.

Upon visiting these colleges, the researchers were impressed by their unique character. College officials have little doubt about their institution's mission. Moreover, the students concur wholeheartedly in support of these goals. For example, during one college visit, the students were holding an international missionary festival. At several colleges, there were daily chapel services, which were voluntarily, and heavily attended. Asked to select the most attractive feature of their college (CUES Local Option Question), 45% of the students chose "religious atmosphere" (n = 475). Fewer than 10% of the students at the other study colleges made this selection. Clearly these colleges have a special environment—one that is reflected in their CUES profiles.

Protestant-Change Colleges

By contrast, the median Protestant-change colleges show a markedly different profile in the 1960's from that of all study colleges and from that of the Protestant colleges. This clear dif-

## Figure 2

## CUES SUMMARY PROFILES: PROTESTANT COLLEGES

Number of students (1960's) = 733
Number of students (1975-6) = 543
Number of institutions = 7

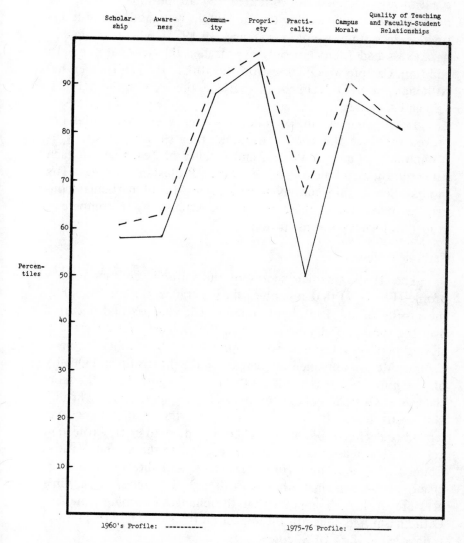

This profile format is adapted from the CUES, Second Edition Technical Manual. Published by:
Institutional Research Program for Higher Education, Educational Testing Service, Princeton, N.J.

ference supports the contention that these six colleges were not similar to the Protestant colleges at the beginning of the study period, having drifted from their Protestant heritage during the late 1950's or early 1960's.[3]

It appears that in the middle 1960's these colleges were reasonably cohesive and friendly institutions but were not primarily academically inclined nor oriented toward personal, poetic, or political reflection (see Figure 3). Morale was modest and a distinctive decorum was not in evidence. By 1975-76 Scholarship and Awareness had risen—but only approached the national norm. In addition, Campus Morale rose from the 50th to the 72nd percentile. Although the SED declined, this reflects the increases in Scholarship and Awareness.

To summarize, these colleges evidence environmental improvement since the 1960's. Although they show some strengths (Community, Campus Morale, and Quality of Teaching), in each category they fall below those of the Protestant colleges. The modest Scholarship and Awareness scores are of particular concern because most of these colleges are attempting to compete as academically superior institutions.

Catholic Colleges

The 1960's median scores of the Catholic colleges form a profile (Figure 4) that resembles the general profile and resembles the profile of the Protestant colleges. The changes that occurred over the time period were similar to the changes that occurred at all study colleges: Community, Propriety, and Practicality declined; Campus Morale remained unchanged; and Scholarship and Quality of Teaching rose. It is significant that the magnitude of the score changes at Catholic colleges exceeded those experienced by Protestant institutions. It is also noteworthy that Catholic colleges tended to decline more on the religiosity index than did Protestant colleges. The reason cited was the reaction to the Second Vatican Council, the encyclical *Humanae Vitae*, and the socioeconomic changes of American Catholics. Although the precise causal linkages are unclear, it appears that the changes sweeping American Catholicism had a significant impact on their colleges. This impact is revealed in the CUES scores.

## Figure 3

# CUES SUMMARY PROFILES: PROTESTANT-CHANGE COLLEGES

Number of students (1960's) = 615
Number of students (1975-6) = 310
Number of institutions = 6

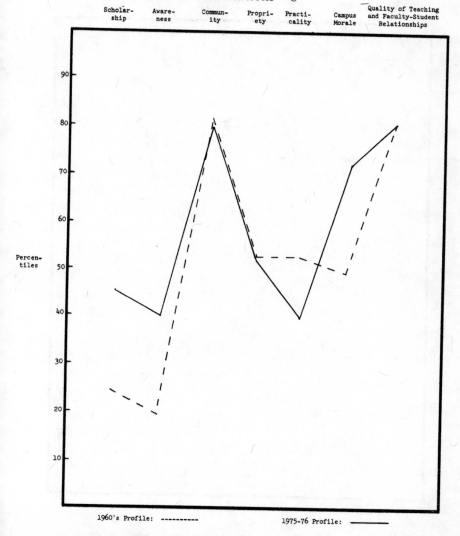

1960's Profile: ----------          1975-76 Profile: _____

This profile format is adapted from the CUES, Second Edition Technical Manual. Published by:
Institutional Research Program for Higher Education, Educational Testing Service, Princeton, N.J.

## Figure 4

### CUES SUMMARY PROFILES: CATHOLIC COLLEGES

Number of students (1960's) = 1584
Number of students (1975-6) = 1206
Number of institutions = 12

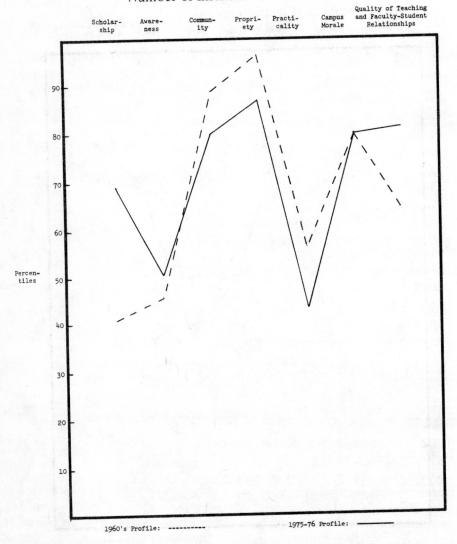

This profile format is adapted from the CUES, Second Edition Technical Manual. Published by: Institutional Research Program for Higher Education, Educational Testing Service, Princeton, N.J.

The SED for the Catholic colleges fell from 5.167 to 3.186. This 37% drop is comparable to that of the Protestant colleges and to that of all study colleges. The decline is primarily attributable to the drop in median Propriety scores.

Catholic-Change Colleges

The similarity of the 1960's Catholic-change profile to the profile for all study colleges is illustrated in Figure 5. The 1960's Catholic-change profile is also quite similar to the 1960's Catholic college profile, although the median Community and Propriety scores are slightly lower and the median Scholarship and Quality of Teaching scores are a little higher for the change colleges. These very modest differences perhaps presage the different policies these two groups of institutions will pursue.

By 1975-76, the median Campus Morale score at the change colleges had fallen 24 percentile points. The median Community score had dropped 21 percentile points. The differences between the two groups of Catholic-heritage colleges are quite important. Although the median Scholarship and Quality of Teaching scores rose at the Catholic colleges, they showed no perceptible movement at the change institutions.

The contrasts between Catholic and Catholic-change colleges appear certain and dramatic. Evaluating the data on a college-by-college basis or on an item-by-item basis further reinforces these results. A review of the campus visits also affirms these findings, but not so completely. That is, the distinctions between a Catholic and a Catholic-change college were not as obvious as they were at Protestant and Protestant-change colleges. In addition, although the mood on the Catholic colleges appeared more optimistic than at the change colleges, the observed differences were not as great as the Community and Campus Morale scores would indicate. But after considering all the data for the 23 colleges with Catholic heritage, it is clear that those labeled Catholic-change evidenced greated environmental deterioration.

## Results Grouped by Sex Composition of the Student Bodies

Female Colleges

The profile of median CUES scores for female college is simi-

## Figure 5

## CUES SUMMARY PROFILES: CATHOLIC-CHANGE COLLEGES

Number of students (1960's) = 843
Number of students (1975-6) = 839
Number of institutions = 11

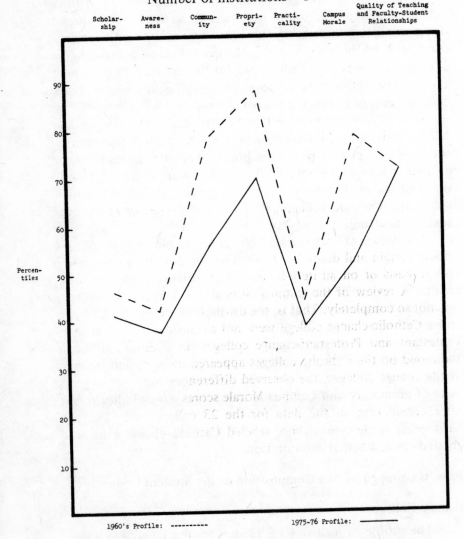

1960's Profile: ----------          1975-76 Profile: ————————

This profile format is adapted from the CUES, Second Edition Technical Manual. Published by: Institutional Research Program for Higher Education, Educational Testing Service, Princeton, N.J.

lar to those of all study colleges (see Figure 6). In the 1960's, the median scores for the female institutions were slightly higher on the Awareness, Community, Propriety, and Campus Morale scales —but not that much higher to alter the general profile. The greatest difference is on the Awareness scale. Again, an item analysis provides some insight. Respondents from the female colleges were more likely to answer in the keyed direction on 16 of the 20 questions; the greatest difference occurred on those items that probe the prominence of fine arts on the campus.

In addition, the profile changes of the median female colleges are very similar to the changes of the median for all colleges. There are declines in Community, Campus Morale, Propriety, and Practicality. There are gains on the Scholarship and Quality of Teaching scale (both increases are somewhat larger than those for all study colleges). Also, the median female institution registered a modest gain in Awareness. The changes are too slight to warrant much attention, however.

An examination of the SED's in Table 8 shows that these institutions initially exhibited a high degree of distinctiveness on this measure (6.228 versus 3.377 for all colleges). Moreover, these colleges declined modestly; the 1975-76 SED was 4.872, a 22% drop.

## Female-Change Colleges

Female institutions that become coeducational after the first administration of CUES had a median profile in the 1960's (Figure 7) that was similar to the profile of all study colleges, the profile of Catholic-change colleges, and the profile of female colleges. Comparing this early profile in detail with that of the female colleges, it is clear that Scholarship was somewhat higher at the female-change colleges (18 percentile points). The major difference appeared on the Practicality scale, where the median female-change colleges scored 27 percentile points below the median female college. An item analysis yielded little insight. Differences were visible but unaccompanied by perceptible patterns. For example, the largest difference occurred on item 5. At the female colleges nearly 72% indicated that "students take great pride in their appearance"; this compared with a 29% response at female-

## Figure 6

## CUES SUMMARY PROFILES: FEMALE COLLEGES

Number of students (1960's) = 1465
Number of students (1975-6) = 1027
Number of institutions = 13

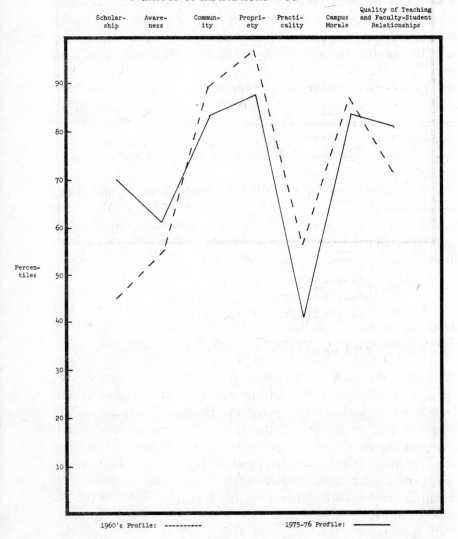

1960's Profile: ----------    1975-76 Profile: ————

This profile format is adapted from the CUES, Second Edition Technical Manual. Published by:
Institutional Research Program for Higher Education, Educational Testing Service, Princeton, N.J.

# Figure 7

## CUES SUMMARY PROFILES: FEMALE-CHANGE COLLEGES

Number of students (1960's) = 285
Number of students (1975- 6) = 343
Number of institutions = 5

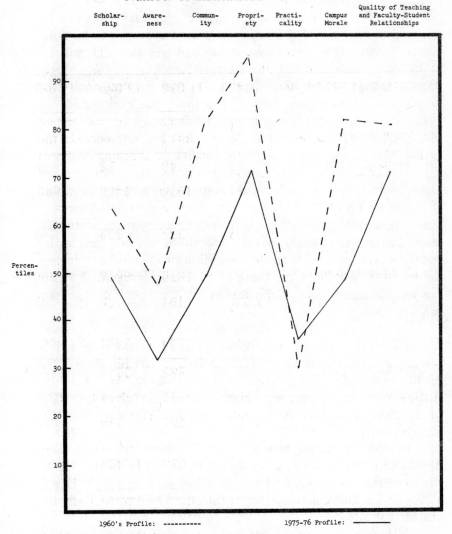

| Scholar-ship | Aware-ness | Commun-ity | Propri-ety | Practi-cality | Campus Morale | Quality of Teaching and Faculty-Student Relationships |

Percen-tiles

1960's Profile: ----------          1975-76 Profile: ————

This profile format is adapted from the CUES, Second Edition Technical Manual. Published by:
Institutional Research Program for Higher Education, Educational Testing Service, Princeton, N.J.

change colleges. No conclusion of a general malaise at the incipient change institutions can be drawn from this response because the community and campus Morale scores were not much lower in the 1960's and certainly well above the computed norm. Item 2 indicated that college events at the median female-change college were more likely to draw a large crowd than they were at the female colleges (72% versus 51%).

With the above exceptions, the colleges that subsequently adopted a coeducational admissions policy appeared to be quite similar in the 1960's to those female colleges that did not. By 1975-76, at least 10% of the students enrolling at the colleges labeled female-change were male; the median full-time-equivalent enrollment of men was 28% of the total. An examination of Figure 7 reveals a rather significant profile change. In contrast to all colleges, and in contrast to female colleges in particular, the median scores for Scholarship and Quality of Teaching declined. The former declined 15 percentile points and the latter dropped eight. Moreover, Community and Campus Morale each plummeted from above the 80th to below the 50th percentiles. Propriety fell 28 percentile points. When these profile changes are contrasted with the profile changes at the Catholic-change colleges, an interesting fact appears. With the exception of Practicality, changes are in the same direction for each scale, but magnified at the female-change colleges. Comparisons of percentile changes are given in Table 9.

CUES is purportedly unaffected by the personal characteristics of students.[4] Nonetheless, these colleges were also scored after removing male respondents. This additional control altered the profile very little. The greatest correction was on the Awareness scale; it rose only six percentile points with males excluded. Quality of Teaching rose four percentile points and Propriety one percentile point.

In addition to the change in profile shape, there is a large decline in distinctiveness, as measured by the SED. In the 1960's this statistic was 6.447. In 1975-76 it had sunk to 1.710. This is a 73% decline (considerably greater than the 53% drop for Catholic-change institutions).

Although some presidents hailed the change to coeducation

## Table 9

## A COMPARISON OF PERCENTILE CHANGES

|  | Scholar-ship | Aware-ness | Com-munity | Pro-priety | Practi-cality | Cam-pus Morale | Quality of Teach-ing |
|---|---|---|---|---|---|---|---|
| All colleges | +13 | +2 | -6 | -10 | -10 | -3 | +5 |
| Catholic-change | -4 | -1 | -21 | -16 | -4 | -24 | 0 |
| Female-change | -15 | -15 | -32 | -23 | +9 | -33 | -8 |
| Female | +24 | +6 | -6 | -9 | -13 | -5 | +10 |

at their colleges, the statement of most campus officials confirmed the findings of this study. According to the reports of these officials, the males were likely to be commuter students, with less academic ability. Moreover, the admission of men did not appear to improve the social environment; when asked to select the least attractive characteristic of their college (CUES Local Option Question), 30% of the respondents at female-change colleges selected "social life" versus 16% at female colleges (n = 343 and 960, respectively). In sum, the evidence suggests that the change to co-education had serious and undesirable environmental consequences at the hitherto female colleges.

## Male-Change Colleges

The six male colleges that admitted women had an altogether different median profile from the median profile for all 40 colleges in the study. The median male-change college was lower in every cateogry on the 1960's CUES administration. Figure 8 shows that the scores were much closer to the median scores of the 100 institutions used to norm the scales; the SED for these colleges was only 0.801 in the 1960's.

After women were admitted, the profile became slightly closer to that of the median college for the whole study group. The Scholarship score increased greatly, as did the Campus Morale

## Figure 8

### CUES SUMMARY PROFILES: MALE-CHANGE COLLEGES

Number of students (1960's) = 885
Number of students (1975-6) = 644
Number of institutions = 6

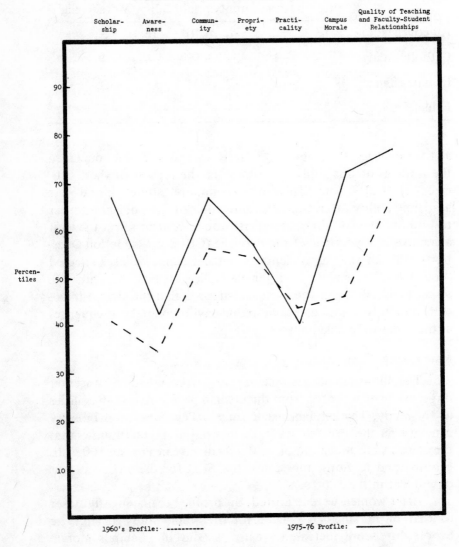

This profile format is adapted from the CUES, Second Edition Technical Manual. Published by:
Institutional Research Program for Higher Education, Educational Testing Service, Princeton, N.J.

score. The median Awareness, Community, and Quality of Teaching scores also registered modest gains. Propriety and Practicality remained essentially unchanged. When female respondents are excluded, the profile change is moderated slightly for this subgroup. The median Community and Campus Morale scores are about six percentile points lower without female respondents. The median Awareness score is slightly higher when women are exluded. None of these differences is so dramatic, however, as to alter significantly the conclusion that the policy to admit women at these heretofore previously all male campuses was environmentally successful. There are gains on all scales except Practicality, and the new profile is apparently more distinctive. The SED rose from 0.801 in the 1960's to 1.178 in 1975-76, up 47%. This success is confirmed by the impressions of administrators, who uniformly praised the change to coeducation.

## Summary

The colleges in this study tended to have remarkably similar profiles in the 1960's. The high scores on Community, Campus Morale, and Quality of Teaching reflected closely-knit campuses with high spirit. The particularly high scores on Propriety indicated a decorous, well-mannered, and orderly environment. Although the schools and their students were not particularly scholarly and discerning, as evidenced by the middle-range Scholarship and Awareness scores, these colleges were oriented toward teaching and were rated highly on this. The slightly above average Practicality score suggested an environment with a modest degress of order and organization but not overly structured.

In 1975-76, this description was still appropriate. Four of the median scores on the seven scales declined, but none more than 12 percentile points. Community and Campus Morale declined by six and three percentile points, respectively; Propriety dropped ten percentile points. In sum, the evidence of the CUES surveys is that these colleges have environments today that are similar to environments of the 1960's. Although campus ambience is apparently less personal and decorous, there seems to be more emphasis placed on teaching and scholarship.

The seven Protestant colleges exhibited a profile that paralleled, although at a somewhat higher level, the profile of all colleges. In 1975-76, this profile retained its shape and, with the exception of the drop in Practicality, it had essentially retained its level. The environment of these colleges remains unique. As measured by CUES, the high sense of community, the campus spirit, and the excellent student-faculty relationships must be considered valuable assets.

The profile of the Protestant-change colleges was distinctly different from the profile of Protestant colleges and from that of all study colleges. The differences between the Protestant-change and Protestant profiles are further evidence that these two groups of colleges were already pursuing distinctly different missions at the beginning of the study period in 1965. This fact tempers conclusions from these data about the impact of secularization at Protestant-heritage colleges. It is significant, however, that in every category the scores of the Protestant-change colleges are below those of the Protestant colleges. Because most of the Protestant-change colleges are attempting to compete as academically superior institutions, the modest Awareness and Scholarship scores are of real concern.

The 12 Catholic and 11 Catholic-change colleges initially showed similar profiles, and both paralleled the profile for all study colleges. In 1975-76, the changes that occurred in the Catholic college profile were similar to the changes at all study colleges—increases in Scholarship and Quality of Teaching, and slight drops in Community and Propriety. On the other hand, the Catholic-change colleges suffered significantly greater declines in Community and Propriety. The median Campus Morale score fell 24 percentile points, whereas the median Scholarship and Quality of Teaching scores did not increase to the same extent as at Catholic colleges. Although these changes cannot be directly attributed to religious policies, they serve as corroboration that the environment of these Catholic-change colleges has been strained.

Examining the results by the sex composition of the student bodies, the results are equally provocative. The 13 female and five female-change colleges exhibited median profiles that were quite similar to the general profile. In 1975-76, the changes that occurred in the female college profile tended to parallel the changes on the profile of all study colleges. But the profile for female-change colleges has altered noticeably with only the Practicality score rising. The other scores dropped markedly. Campus Morale and Community showed the largest decline, 33 and 32 percentile points, respectively. Removing the responses of males made no significant difference. And although each of the female colleges was also categorized as a Catholic-change college, the changes are much more pronounced than for the larger Catholic-change subgroup. The conclusion must be that change from a female-only admissions policy to coeducation had an additional, and deleterious, impact on campus ambience.

The profile of medians for the six male-change colleges was quite different from the profile of all colleges. All the early median scores fell within the middle third of the national score range. Thus, although these colleges were unique in that they were single-sex, their CUES profile was not particularly distinctive. By 1975-76, the median scores, except Practicality, rose; Scholarship and Campus Morale increased about 25 percentile points each. Although this study cannot attribute these increases directly to the coeducational admissions policies, the evidence is that coeducation was environmentally successful at hitherto male colleges.

The Summary Estimate of Distinctiveness measures declined for all subgroups except the six male-change colleges. The declines were, however, most noticeable at Catholic-change colleges and female-change colleges. This evidence suggests a general decline in distinctiveness of these special purpose colleges and supports the impressions obtained by visually inspecting the CUES charts. The loss of distinctiveness must be of great concern to administrators at these colleges. If these institutions do not offer a unique education, students will be reluctant to pay their relatively higher tuition charges.

## Chapter 4

# Financial/Operating Results

This chapter, as the preceding one, is divided into three sections. The first section reviews ten-year results of operations for all the sample colleges in detail. The second section analyzes the results of operations of institutions grouped by religious orientation, and the third section examines the colleges grouped by sex composition of their student bodies.

## All Sample Institutions

### Demand for the Product

Because tuition represents approximately two-thirds of the total revenue of the sample institutions, enrollment is obviously a critical concern. Row $a$ of Table 10 shows clearly the increase in average full-time-equivalent students during the 1960's and the subsequent leveling in the 1970's. But colleges, unlike many businesses, are concerned not only about the volume of sales, but also about who buys and why. If they consider themselves academically selective, they are concerned with the quality of their applicants and enrolling students. Row $b$ of Table 10 shows that the average number of applications for places in the freshman class rose steadily (at an annualized rate of 1%) until 1972, with a subsequent decline (3% annualized rate). Part of the enrollment increases and resistance to decline can be attributed to an apparently more open admissions policy (see row $c$); the percentage of applicants accepted has increased steadily from 72% to 84%. Although one might explain this increasing receptivity as a manifestation of a more focused

**Table 10**

**DEMAND: AVERAGE FOR ALL STUDY COLLEGES**

|  | | 1965 | 1968 | 1972 | 1975 |
|---|---|---|---|---|---|
| a. | F.T.E. enrollment | 920 | 1068 | 1144 | 1146 |
| b. | Applications | 655 | 666 | 683 | 619 |
| c. | % Accepted | 72 | 77 | 81 | 84 |
| d. | % Choosing to enroll | 67 | 66 | 64 | 65 |
| e. | # Enrolling | 264 | 285 | 305 | 301 |
| f. | SAT scores (average verbal and math) | 522 | 505 | 489 | 472 |
| g. | % Receiving financial aid | 33 | 40 | 50 | 57 |
| h. | % Commuting students | 33 | 32 | 33 | 34 |
| i. | % Coming from out-of-state | 37 | 37 | 37 | 34 |
| j. | % Students over age 25 | 4 | 5 | 6 | 9 |

and successful recruiting effort, there has been a parallel and steady fall in average entering Scholastic Aptitude Test scores.[1] The drop of 10% shown in row *f* is somewhat higher than the 6% national decline.[2] On an annualized basis, the change is slightly more than 1% for the study colleges and slightly more than ½% for all test takers. In a positive sense, the percent of accepted applicants choosing to enroll, given in row *d*, is high and has been relatively stable over this ten-year period.

Rows *h* through *j* of Table 10 detail other trends. If these colleges view a diverse and residential student body as worthwhile to their educational mission, then it is important and advantageous that the percent of out-of-state students has declined little and that the percent of commuting students has risen only one percentage point. There has been a marked increase in the number of adults attending these colleges. Indeed, most administrators with whom the researchers spoke have indicated a strong interest in tapping the continuing education market.

Finally, one may observe in row *g* that the average percent of students receiving financial aid rose rapidly from 33% to 57%. Considering that tuition finances almost two-thirds of the educational and general budget, this trend is quite important and warrants watching.

On balance, enrollments at these institutions appear to have stabilized after a significant increase in the 1960's. The total 25% enrollment increase occurred, however, during a period in which enrollments almost doubled nationally. Trends in acceptance rates and SAT scores suggest that these institutions may have achieved even these enrollment levels with some difficulty.

Notes on Summary Finance Tables

Table 11 details a consolidated average balance sheet for the sample colleges; Table 12 presents the same data on a per student basis. (The rationale for consolidating balance sheet information is discussed in Chapter 2.)

Table 16 is the average current fund income and expense statement adjusted for price increases; this information is presented on a per student basis in Table 17. The income data are not in the standard reporting format because of difficulties in interpreting the many non-standard reports of the colleges.

In addition, frequent reference will be made to selected average ratios; debt as a percent of equity is an example. The average ratio is not equal to the ratio of average debt to average equity because all institutions in the sample affect the first statistic equally, whereas this is not necessarily true for the second statistic.[3] A weighting system to resolve this discrepancy was discarded as unnecessary. When there are significant variations between colleges, disaggregated data are reviewed and reported.

Liquidity

Rows *a* and *e* of Tables 11 and 12 show the trends in average liquid assets and short-term debt for the sample colleges. These data indicate that the latter have been rising faster than the former. But the statistics of Table 13 provide more direct evidence. For

## Table 11

### AVERAGE CONSOLIDATED BALANCE SHEET: ALL COLLEGES[a]

|  | 1965 | 1968 | 1972 | 1975 |
|---|---|---|---|---|
| *Assests* | | | | |
| a.  Liquid assets | 1793 | 2194 | 2606 | 3029 |
| b.  Other assets | 745 | 1014 | 1713 | 2096 |
| c.  Plant assets | 6426 | 8574 | 10,620 | 12,042 |
| d.  Total assets | 8964 | 11,782 | 14,939 | 17,167 |
| *Debt* | | | | |
| e.  Short-term debt | 149 | 216 | 388 | 478 |
| f.  Other debt | 357 | 574 | 1000 | 1175 |
| g.  Long-term debt | 1348 | 2012 | 2572 | 2933 |
| h.  Total debt | 1854 | 2802 | 3960 | 4586 |
| *Equity* | | | | |
| i.  Current fund balance | 208 | 204 | 86 | 105 |
| j   Investment in plant | 4956 | 6269 | 7637 | 8925 |
| k.  Other equity in plant fund | 160 | 356 | 380 | 437 |
| l.  Endowment fund balance | 1739 | 2109 | 2814 | 3025 |
| m. Loan fund balance | 47 | 42 | 62 | 89 |
| n.  Total equity | 7110 | 8980 | 10,979 | 12,581 |
| o.  Total debt and equity | 8964 | 11,782 | 14,939 | 17,167 |

[a]All dollars in thousands.

**Table 12**

**CONSOLIDATED BALANCE SHEET PER STUDENT:
ALL COLLEGES**

|  | 1965 | 1968 | 1972 | 1975 |
|---|---|---|---|---|
| *Assets* | | | | |
| a.  Liquid assets | 1949 | 2055 | 2278 | 2644 |
| b.  Other assets | 810 | 950 | 1498 | 1829 |
| c.  Plant assets | 6986 | 8031 | 9283 | 10,510 |
| d.  Total assets | 9745 | 11,036 | 13,059 | 14,983 |
| *Debt* | | | | |
| e.  Short-term debt | 162 | 202 | 339 | 417 |
| f.  Other debt | 389 | 537 | 874 | 1026 |
| g.  Long-term debt | 1465 | 1885 | 2248 | 2559 |
| h.  Total debt | 2016 | 2624 | 3461 | 4002 |
| *Equity* | | | | |
| i.  Current fund balance | 226 | 191 | 75 | 92 |
| j.  Investment in plant | 5387 | 5872 | 6676 | 7790 |
| k.  Other equity in plant fund | 201 | 333 | 332 | 381 |
| l.  Endowment fund balance | 1891 | 1976 | 2460 | 2640 |
| m.  Loan fund balance | 51 | 40 | 55 | 78 |
| n.  Total equity | 7729 | 8412 | 9598 | 10,981 |
| o.  Total debt and equity | 9745 | 11,036 | 13,059 | 14,983 |

example, row *a* shows the trend in average "liquid ratios." Although the decline from 78 to 13 on this measure is dramatic, the use of an average may be misleading. Row *b* indicates the percents of institutions that could not meet short-term creditors with readily available assets (including endowment) at the end of the designated fiscal years. After a marked increase from 1968 to 1972, there is a decline in 1975. If endowment funds are excluded, as they are for the percentages in row *c*, the trend is more regular and the percent unable to meet conceivable creditor demands rise constantly.

Which trend is more revealing? A case can be made for either. The inclusion of endowment, it can be argued, is more meaningful because these funds can, in fact, be liquidated, borrowed, or used as collateral to meet the demands of short-term creditors. Or, it may be posited, these funds should be excluded in this report because the data on endowment funds represent book, not market, value. Moreover, information from about half the institutions indicates a serious erosion of endowment market value from 1972 to 1975. This report takes the position that the *trend* arrayed in row *c* of Table 13 (i.e., endowment excluded) is closer to fact—cash flow problems are becoming increasingly more prevalent. The *percentage* of colleges that had fewer cash or near-cash assets than pressing debts, however, is better illuminated in row *b* (i.e., endowment included). Thus, in 1975, approximately 15% to 20% of small private colleges, similar to the study colleges, could not meet short-term debt with available assets at the end of their fiscal years—typically June 30th.

To refine this discussion further, one additional point should be made. Summer is typically the season when short-term debt accumulates and revenues are slack. Colleges hold considerably more cash relative to debt after the fall term commences. Yet, they hold even less cash relative to debt at the end of the summer.

The final indicator, the average of short-term debt as a percent of current fund income (row *d*), has increased since 1965. This trend provides additional evidence of the growing significance of short-term debt.

To summarize these data, there is a significant cash flow problem at at least 15% of these institutions. The incidence of

## Table 13

### LIQUIDITY: ALL INSTITUTIONS

|  | 1965 | 1968 | 1972 | 1975 |
|---|---|---|---|---|
| a.  Average "liquid ratio" | 78 | 85 | 31 | 13 |
| b.  Percent of institutions with<br>"liquid ratio" < 1 | 10% | 10% | 22% | 15% |
| (N) | (4) | (4) | (9) | (6) |
| c.  Percent of institutions with<br>"liquid ratio" < 1 with endow-<br>ment excluded | 43% | 45% | 55% | 63% |
| (N) | (17) | (18) | (22) | (25) |
| d.  Average short-term debt as<br>a percent of current fund income | 9% | 8% | 12% | 11% |

liquidity problems over ten years has been increasing. Based on discussions with business managers at these colleges, it seems that the underlying structure of the summer cash flow is not improving. Rather, the business managers are becoming technically more proficient in dealing with the problems (e.g., borrowing later in the summer term).

Debt Structure

The average consolidated balance sheets show total debt increasing faster than total equity. This trend is examined in greater detail in Table 14. Using debt/equity as a measure of the debt structure of these institutions, row *a* reveals a steady, but modest, increase in the average debt position of these colleges from 1965 to 1972, with the measure stabilizing after 1972. However, row *b* indicates that debt as a percentage of income is lower in 1975 than in any of the prior years under study.

Returning to Tables 11 and 12, one sees a modest reordering of the type of debt incurred. The relative decline of long-term debt represents an end to the building boom and more rapid increases in other forms of debt. Short-term debt has increased

## Table 14

### DEBT: ALL INSTITUTIONS

|  | 1965 | 1968 | 1972 | 1975 |
|---|---|---|---|---|
| a. Debt/Equity | 43% | 46% | 50% | 50% |
| b. Total debt/Current income | 111% | 115% | 120% | 102% |
| c. Debt payments/Current income | 5.2% | 4.7% | 4.7% | 5.6% |

absolutely and relatively because of increasing difficulty in meeting summer cash needs.

Finally, row *c* of Table 14 reveals a decline and then an increase in debt payments relative to income during the ten-year period. The recent increase reflects the previous use of loan agreements in which the rate of repayment increases with time. Business managers typically indicated that their college's payments would be growing during the coming decades because of such provisions.

The average insitutition has significantly increased its debt since 1965; the rate of increase leveled off after 1972. The reality of this statistical trend was reinforced by discussions with campus officials; most colleges report that they are incurring new debt with considerable caution. There are counter examples, however. When questioned about a new building financed primarily with debt one president remarked: "I don't see retrenchment as a solution to the financial problems of the 1970's. . . . If we go down it will be with our flag flying." More common was the business manager who noted: "The only new debt we will take on is summer borrowing, to see us through until September." Indeed, short-term borrowing has been increasing. It appears, however, that the cash flow problem is of more immediate concern than the trend in total debt. The cash flow trend is closely related to operating results, a topic that will be discussed below.

Financial Resources

To review the rationale detailed in Chapter 2, it is believed that equity, or net worth, is an important measure of the financial trends of private colleges. Equity, as a measure of ownership, represents the resources an institution can bring to bear on the education of students. Total equity is thus more important than total assets because the assets may be funded with debt and, of course, the principal and interest of the debts must be repaid. This debt service acts as a drain on current fund income.

Rows $i$ through $m$ of Tables 11 and 12 summarize the changes in fund balances for the average sample institution. With the exception of the current fund, the trends are nearly uniformly upward. The large gain in the plant fund is not unexpected. Spurred on by rising enrollments and low-interest federal loans, most of these colleges increased their plant rapidly in the 1960's. Mandatory repayment schedules ensure the repayment of plant debt with concurrent accretion of plant equity. The size of the increase in endowment was not fully anticipated. As previously noted, however, the trend in book value does not necessarily mirror the trend in market value. For nearly half the institutions, there was information on market values. These data reveal a rapid rise from 1965 to 1972 and an equally swift decline from 1972 to 1975.

Although current fund equity is a minor portion of total equity, it is significant that it has declined so rapidly. In 1965, 12% of the study colleges had negative current fund balances. By 1975, this figure had risen to 38%. To some extent, this difference may represent a random reassignment of funds from one group to another. On the other hand, this change may parallel, and be symptomatic of, cash flow problems. That is, it is becoming increasingly more likely that at the end of the year there are not enough assets in the current fund to meet current obligations.

Table 15 presents other selected measures of resource growth at the sample institutions. Row $a$ shows a consistent increase in average equity, totaling 77%, or 6% per year. The next row corrects the data for enrollment changes. Still, the net worth, or equity, grows at 4% per year. In answer to the obvious question about the impact of declining enrollments on this trend, row $c$ presents the same data but excludes colleges in the sample whose enrollments declined during the 1965 to 1975 period. Again the trend is up and the annualized rate of increase is 3%, emphasizing that most of the gain was *not* a result of declining enrollments. Additionally

## Table 15

### GROWTH IN RESOURCES: ALL COLLEGES
(N = 40)

| | 1965 | 1968 | 1972 | 1975 | Annual-ized % Increase |
|---|---|---|---|---|---|
| a. Average total equity (in $1000's) | 7110 | 8980 | 10,979 | 12,581 | 6% |
| b. Average total equity per student | 7729 | 8412 | 9597 | 10,980 | 4% |
| c. Average total equity per student: colleges without enrollment declines | 7955 | 8543 | 9739 | 10,637 | 3% |
| d. Average total equity per student after estimating depreciation | 7729 | 7849 | 8168 | 8809 | 1% |

one should ask: How does the generally accepted, but potentially misleading, accounting practice of reporting plant assets at book value without depreciation affect this trend? Row *d* deducts from the total equity an estimate for depreciation of plant (assuming a 40-year life). With this adjustment the rate of increase is greatly reduced—to an annualized rate of just over 1%. This last estimate is probably the most accurate. It suggests that resources per student, on average, have increased slightly. But considering the assumptions, this small increase is not comforting. Moreover, this is an average increase and includes colleges at which enrollments have declined.

## Operating Results

This analysis relies to a large measure on current fund income and expense data. Table 16 displays these data averaged on a per college basis and adjusted for price increases. Table 17 presents the same categories of information per student.

*Income.* The term "externally controlled income" refers to income the college does not control—essentially gifts and grants from public and private sources. Tuition is considered separately. By separately aggregating investment income, contributed services, and "other internal income," the total current fund income is subdivided into (1) tuition, (2) externally controlled income, and (3) internally controlled income. By examining the trends in relative support from these three sources, one can make some determinations as to the potential changes in influence on this group of institutions. Figure 9 presents the trends of these three sources as a percent of educational and general income.

Tuition as a percent of educational and general income has been relatively stable over the ten-year study period. Inspecting absolute tuition in Table 16, one sees an increase from an average of $1,586,000 per institution to $2,372,000 per institution (both 1975 dollars). Because enrollments have all also risen, however, the per student tuition revenue (a reasonable approximation for tuition charges) has risen less sharply. The increase from $1,726 to $2,070 indicates nonetheless that revenue per student from this source is rising faster than prices. The rise to $2,070 represents an 8% annualized accretion. The consumer price index rose only a 5¼% annually.

In contrast to tuition, there has been a constant decline in internally generated income as a percent of educational and general revenue accompanied by a rise in externally generated income. Most of the decline represents the loss of contributed services at Roman Catholic colleges. The remainder is a relative decline in investment income as a source of support. The decline occured for two reasons—inflation and enrollment increases. One sees in row *c* of Table 16 that total investment income increased more rapidly

## Table 16

**CURRENT FUND INCOME AND EXPENDITURES:
ALL COLLEGES[a]**

|  | 1965 | 1968 | 1972 | 1975 |
|---|---|---|---|---|
| *Income* | | | | |
| a. Tuition | 1586 | 2062 | 2330 | 2372 |
| b. Outside income | 299 | 462 | 557 | 798 |
| c. Investment income | 143 | 158 | 164 | 173 |
| d. Contributed services | 235 | 232 | 180 | 138 |
| e. Other internal income | 88 | 56 | 28 | 114 |
| f. Educational and general | 2351 | 2970 | 3259 | 3595 |
| g. Auxiliary services | 900 | 1054 | 964 | 940 |
| h. Total current fund income | 3251 | 4024 | 4223 | 4535 |
| *Expenditures* | | | | |
| i. Instructional expenditures | 1036 | 1303 | 1360 | 1371 |
| j. Administration | 255 | 312 | 319 | 350 |
| k. Library | 110 | 152 | 155 | 168 |
| l. Maintenance | 288 | 343 | 371 | 402 |
| m. Student services | 191 | 238 | 270 | 306 |
| n. Student aid | 204 | 288 | 326 | 372 |
| o. Sponsored programs and research | 37 | 75 | 158 | 167 |
| p. Other expenditures | 211 | 272 | 254 | 353 |
| q. Total educational and general expenditures | 2332 | 2983 | 3213 | 3489 |
| r. Auxiliary services | 752 | 893 | 859 | 843 |
| s. Total current fund expenditures | 3084 | 3876 | 4072 | 4332 |

|                         | 1965 | 1968 | 1972 | 1975 |
|-------------------------|------|------|------|------|
| t. Surplus 1            | 167  | 148  | 151  | 203  |
| u. Mandatory transfers  | 55   | 88   | 106  | 157  |
| v. Surplus 2            | 112  | 60   | 45   | 46   |
| w. Other transfers      | 9    | 60   | 73   | 76   |
| x. Surplus 3            | 103  | 0    | (28) | (30) |

aAll figures in thousands and in constant (1975) dollars.

than inflation. When this is corrected for enrollment (row *c* of Table 17), however, there is a slight decline in investment income per student.

There are several reasons that externally controlled income is rising. One explanation is that it is the result of an accounting change. In 1973, the American Institute of Certified Public Accountants issued an audit guide, which advised that all unrestricted gifts pass through the current fund.[4] Prior to this, it was not uncommon to see the entry "gifts applied to current operations." The implication is that there were other gifts not so applied. The impact of the Audit Guide on this has been confirmed by discussions with business managers. These officers did believe, however, that gift income, regardless of the accounting change, was playing a larger part in their operation. Most important to all these colleges were government operating subsidies, most of which were provided by the state. In those states that offer direct support for private higher education, business managers and presidents would typically note: "That [state support] has made the difference." "We'd be in real trouble without those state dollars." For 31 colleges for which data were available, the average government support rose from 1% to 10%. Even this underestimates the increasing reliance of these colleges on state and federal governments, because these data emcompass only the money that passes through the current fund. A large portion of the recently built plant was financed through grants or loans by the Federal government.

## Table 17

### CURRENT FUND INCOME AND EXPENDITURES PER STUDENT: ALL COLLEGES[a]

|  | 1965 | 1968 | 1972 | 1975 |
|---|---|---|---|---|
| *Income* | | | | |
| a. Tuition | 1726 | 1884 | 1987 | 2070 |
| b. Outside income | 325 | 432 | 488 | 696 |
| c. Investment income | 150 | 141 | 125 | 147 |
| d. Contributed services | 255 | 211 | 153 | 120 |
| e. Other internal income | 101 | 138 | 117 | 105 |
| f. Educational and general | 2557 | 2806 | 2870 | 3138 |
| g. Auxiliary services | 978 | 963 | 822 | 820 |
| h. Total current fund income | 3535 | 3769 | 3692 | 3958 |
| *Expenditures* | | | | |
| i. Instructional expenditures | 1126 | 1190 | 1158 | 1197 |
| j. Administration | 249 | 263 | 258 | 298 |
| k. Library | 117 | 135 | 118 | 136 |
| l. Maintenance | 314 | 313 | 316 | 351 |
| m. Student services | 150 | 183 | 213 | 241 |
| n. Student aid | 211 | 249 | 270 | 325 |
| o. Sponsored programs and research | 26 | 41 | 83 | 105 |
| p. Other expenditures | 339 | 443 | 412 | 393 |
| q. Total educational and general expenditures | 2532 | 2817 | 2828 | 3046 |
| r. Auxiliary services | 818 | 814 | 732 | 735 |
| s. Total current fund expenditures | 3350 | 3631 | 3560 | 3781 |

|                        | 1965 | 1968 | 1972 | 1975 |
|------------------------|------|------|------|------|
| t.  Surplus 1          | 185  | 138  | 132  | 177  |
| u.  Mandatory transfers| 59   | 80   | 90   | 137  |
| v.  Surplus 2          | 126  | 58   | 42   | 40   |
| w.  Other transfers    | 11   | 55   | 62   | 67   |
| x.  Surplus 3          | 115  | 3    | (20) | (27) |

a All figures in constant (1975) dollars.

Furthermore, there are large amounts of student aid that go directly to students.

*Expenses.* Table 18 presents expenditures at the sample institutions as percentages of the total educational and general budget. The most notable trends are the decline in percent of expenditures on instruction and the increase in the percents devoted to student aid, and to sponsored programs and research. Administration, library, maintenance, student services, and other costs have remained stable when measured in this way. But these trends of percentages are of limited use; other factors must be taken into account. Although the average expenditure per student data in Table 16 are useful, Table 19 presents an additional selection of operating statistics. One notes that the student-faculty ratio increased from 14:1 in 1965 and 1968 to 15:1 in 1972 to 16:1 in 1975. One Carnegie Commission report suggested that student faculty ratios, which they indicate to be 14:1 for private liberal arts colleges in 1966,[5] might be cautiously raised.[6] Thus it would seem that these colleges were rather typical in the middle 1960's with regard to student-faculty mix and did, indeed, increase these ratios. Whether the change was cautious cannot be determined here. It is clear, however, that increases in student-faculty ratios cannot continue endlessly.

Examining instructional expenditures per student adjusted for inflation,[7] we observe a total 4% increase from 1965 to 1968, a very slight decline in 1972, and a 2% decline in 1975. One inter-

Figure 9

INCOME SOURCES AS A PERCENT OF EDUCATIONAL AND
GENERAL INCOME: ALL COLLEGES (N = 40)

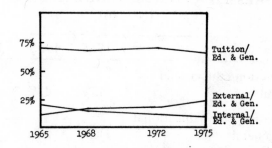

pretation might be that these colleges have eroded the financial strength of their academic program that they gained in the 1960's. An equally plausible explanation is that efficient administrators have cut out the extravagances that accrued during the previous euphoric period. If these colleges have been more efficient vis-à-vis instruction, this is not true for educational and general expenditures as a whole. Average cost per student in this aggregate category, row $f$, have risen 20% more rapidly than the prices. Reviewing subcategories other than instruction, we notice that both administration and student services exceed the growth in prices.

Library expenditures were not adjusted on a per student basis because it was believed that these institutions should have a basic minimum library. A better adjustment might have been per program offered at the college, but this information was not collected. In any event, the data in row $e$ are adjusted for inflation and not enrollments; these expenditures have risen considerably more rapidly than prices.

Maintenance costs listed under educational and general expenditures were corrected for inflation and the size of the plant.[8] Book value of the plant is used as proxy for size because of lack of better information. These data in row $g$ of Table 19 show a consistent decline.

Row $h$ reveals that student aid has been rising as a percent of tuition, from 13% to 18%. Clearly this is an unavoidable problem for these tuition-dependent colleges.

Table 18

EDUCATIONAL AND GENERAL EXPENDITURES
EXPRESSED AS PERCENTAGES: ALL COLLEGES
(N = 40)

|  | | 1965 | 1968 | 1972 | 1975 |
|---|---|---|---|---|---|
| a. | Instruction/educational and general | 45% | 43% | 41% | 39% |
| b. | Administration/educational and general | 12% | 12% | 11% | 11% |
| c. | Library/educational and general | 5% | 5% | 5% | 5% |
| d. | Maintenance/educational and general | 11% | 10% | 10% | 10% |
| e. | Student services/educational and general | 7% | 6% | 7% | 8% |
| f. | Student aid/educational and general | 8% | 9% | 10% | 11% |
| g. | Sponsored programs and research/educational and general | 1% | 2% | 4% | 4% |
| h. | Other expenditure/ educational and general | 11% | 13% | 12% | 12% |
| i. | Total (%) | 100% | 100% | 100% | 100% |

*Note*: Slight variations here from Tables 16 and 17 represent the method of calculating averages for institutions insead of an average aggregate percentage.

*Surpluses and Deficits.* In spite of general reservations about the accuracy of surplus/deficit data, they do provide evidence on the operating position of these colleges. After correcting for inflation and enrollments, we observe that the average study college earned a surplus of $125 per student (1975 dollars) in 1965. This

## Table 19

## SELECTED OPERATIONAL MEASURES: ALL COLLEGES
(N = 40)

|  | | 1965 | 1968 | 1972 | 1975 |
|---|---|---|---|---|---|
| a. | Student-faculty ratio | 14:1 | 14:1 | 15:1 | 16:1 |
| b. | Instructional expenditure/ student (1975 $'s) | $1205 | 1250 | 1245 | 1215 |
| c. | Administrative expenditure/ student (1975 $'s) | $249 | 263 | 258 | 298 |
| d. | Student services expenditure/ student (1975 $'s) | $150 | 183 | 213 | 241 |
| e. | Library expenditures (1975 $'s) | $110,000 | 152,000 | 155,000 | 168,000 |
| f. | Educational & general expenditure/student (1975 $'s) | $2535 | 2816 | 2829 | 3046 |
| g. | Maintenance (1975 $'s)/ plant book value | 4.7% | 4.2% | 3.6% | 3.4% |
| h. | Student aid/ tuition | 12.7% | 15.2% | 16.0% | 18.2% |
| i. | Surplus[a]/ student (1975) | 125 | 58 | 40 | 40 |

|  | 1965 | 1968 | 1972 | 1975 |
|---|---|---|---|---|
| j.  Percent of institutions with operating deficits | 25% | 40% | 48% | 33% |

aSurplus is defined as Current fund income less Expenditures less Mandatory transfers.

*Note*: Slight variations here from Tables 16 and 17 represent the method of calculating averages for institutions instead of an average aggregate percentage.

dropped to $58 in 1968 and then to $40 in 1972. In 1975, the average surplus per student remained at $40. It appears, therefore, that these colleges have recently been able to match cost increases with more income. Another measure is the percent of study colleges showing deficits. Row *j* of Table 19 reveals a pattern not unlike that of the average surplus; the percent of colleges with deficits rose from 25% to 40% to 48%, and then fell to 33% in 1975.

*Summary*. Analysis of the operating position of the 40 study colleges yields a mixed picture. Educational and general costs per student have risen considerably faster than has the price index. This increase has *not* gone into instruction. In fact, there is some evidence that support for the instructional expenditures appears to have been channeled into the library, student aid, administration, and the recruiting effort listed in student services. Maintenance as a percent of plant has also declined. The average surplus remained constant in 1975 after two successive declines.

## Results Grouped by Religious Orientation of the Colleges

This section will concentrate on deviations from patterns set by all study colleges. Graphic summaries are used rather than the more precise, but tedious, tabular forms.

Figure 10 graphs enrollment data. The most direct conclusion that we can draw from this graph is that, when colleges are grouped in this fashion, the trends closely follow the pattern for all study

**Figure 10**

**AVERAGE F.T.E. ENROLLMENT: INSTITUTIONS GROUPED BY RELIGIOUS ORIENTATION**

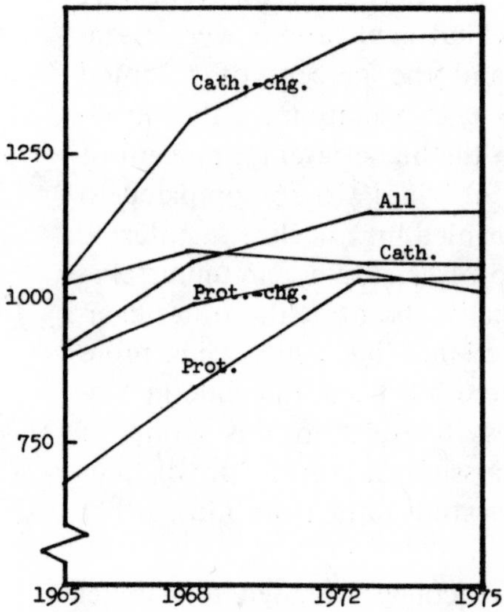

**Figure 11**

**AVERAGE APPLICATIONS: INSTITUTIONS GROUPED BY RELIGIOUS ORIENTATION**

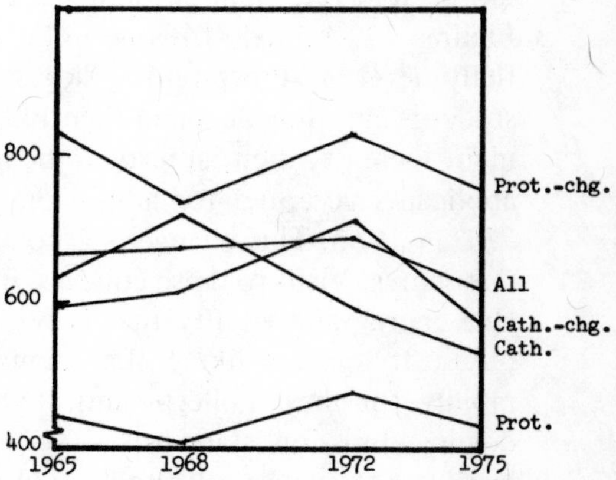

**Figure 12**

**AVERAGE PERCENT OF APPLICANTS ACCEPTED: INSTITUTIONS GROUPED BY RELIGIOUS ORIENTATION**

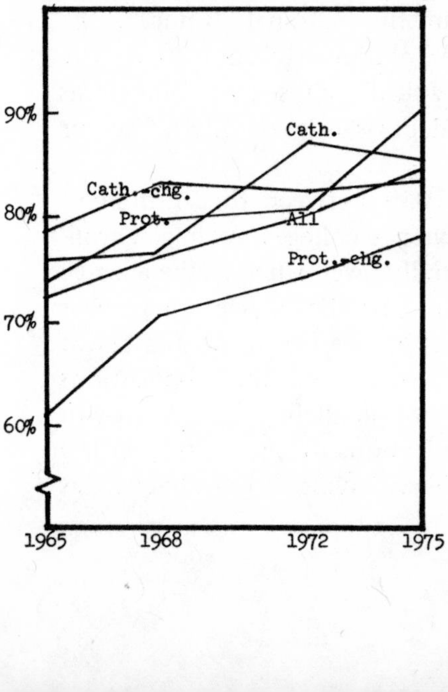

**Figure 13**

**AVERAGE PERCENT OF STUDENTS ACCEPTED WHO ENROLL: INSTITUTIONS GROUPED BY RELIGIOUS ORIENTATION**

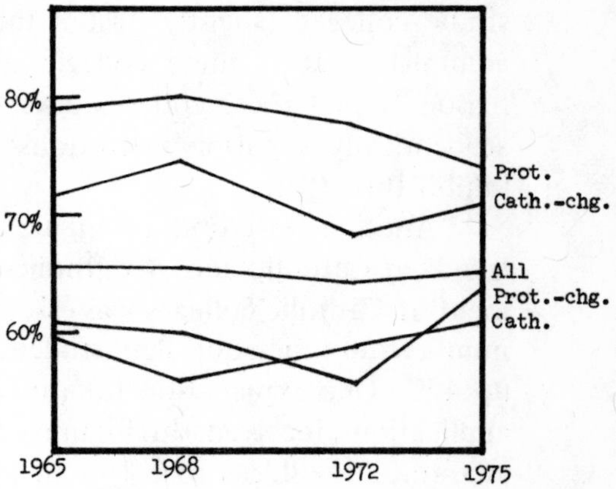

colleges. Most of the sub-groups showed enrollment growth from 1965 to 1972 with characteristic leveling in 1975. There are some differences, however.

Average enrollments at Protestant colleges increased at a more rapid rate than enrollments at all study colleges. Reviewing Figures 11 through 14, one notices that applications were essentially level at Protestant colleges and the percent of accepted students enrolling declined slightly. The explanation for the enrollment increase, then, appears to be in the higher average percent of applicants accepted for admission—90% in 1975-76 compared to 73% in 1965. This change is accompanied by a decline in entering test scores. Visits to these colleges, however, disclose an unmistakeable energy and vitality that is typically absent at the other campuses. It appears likely that demand has been increasing more rapidly for these colleges and, if there has been a decline in academic admission standards, it is less relevant to this group of institutions, whose self-proclaimed missions are decidedly distinct from most other institutions in this study and from most other colleges in America.

Enrollment at Protestant-change colleges tended to parallel enrollments at all study colleges. Since 1972, however, the number of applications received has declined; they have therefore increased their acceptance rate more rapidly than average. In addition, although SAT scores have declined at about the same rate as at all study colleges (slightly faster than the national average), the administrators at these colleges are particularly concerned. The reason is that these colleges have typically chosen to compete as academically superior institutions; depressed levels of SAT scores inhibit this effort.

Another variation in Figure 10 is between the enrollment trends at Catholic and at Catholic-change colleges. Average enrollment at Catholic colleges was essentially level, whereas the average number full-time-equivalent student at Catholic-change colleges was up 42%. One explanation for this difference lies in the number of applications received. In Figure 11, we observe that applications at Catholic colleges rose 14% in 1968, paralleling the 5% growth in students. In following years, applications dropped 26%, with a concurrent decline in enrollment. The decline in enrollment was

**Figure 14**

AVERAGE SAT SCORES: INSTITUTIONS GROUPED
BY RELIGIOUS ORIENTATION

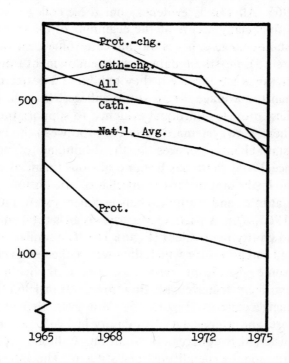

less severe than the decline in applicants, apparently because of an increased rate of acceptance. Over the 1965-1972 period, applications at Catholic-change colleges grew by over 20%. The subsequent reduction in applications was not matched by an enroll-ment decline, but SAT scores fell in parallel fashion. In addition, it should be noted that, at the Catholic-change colleges, commuter students came to represent a larger proportion of the student body —49% in 1975 compared to 41% in 1965. Catholic colleges had a lower percentage of commuter students in 1975 (42%) than they did in 1965 (46%). At the same time, both groups became some-what more dependent upon older students.

One of the clearest patterns to emerge in the financial analysis is that the Protestant-change colleges displayed a financial distinctiveness at the beginning of the study period. In Figure 16 through 19, we note that these colleges showed a lower than average debt, more resources, and expended more money per student on instructions in 1965. All this is evidence that these colleges as a group were more financially secure at the beginning of the study period. The Protestant-change colleges did indicate some cash flow problems (Figure 15), but these data exclude endowment funds. When endowment funds are included, they exhibited a better cash flow position than the average for all study colleges. In sum, the 1965 financial data provide additional evidence to support the contention that there were systematic differences between the Protestant and Protestant-change colleges at the beginning of the study period. Since 1965, there has been no obvious financial advantage to either the Protestant or Protestant-change orientation.

The Catholic and Catholic-change colleges were much more similar in 1965. This is particularly true vis-à-vis total equity (Figure 17) and equity per student (Figure 18). The similarities persist on almost all categories for which data were collected. There were, however, some significant variations. The Catholic institutions were far less likely to have cash flow problems in 1965 than were Catholic-change colleges (Figure 15). Moreover, their debts were more modest, and averaged 49% of equity in 1965, versus 65% for the Catholic-change colleges. In addition, Catholic colleges had lower instructional expenditures per student. The interpretation of this, and one that historians are challenged to verify, is that the Catholic and Catholic-change colleges were indeed quite similar in the 1960's. Catholic-change colleges, however, embarked on a significantly more ambitious expansion program. They bolstered their instructional programs and improved their campuses with debt financing. After the decade was half over, it became apparent that their traditional mission, Catholic education, did not have a sufficiently broad appeal in a changing society to support their ambitious expansion. (Note that long-term debt at the Catholic colleges was $1,200 per student in 1965; at Catholic-change colleges, it was $2,000 per student.) Thus these change institutions sought to expand enrollments with a broadened mission.

Were these policies successful? As noted earlier, enrollments *did* increase. Although the Catholic-change colleges still have a

Figure 15

**PERCENT OF INSTITUTIONS WITH LIQUID RATIO LESS THAN ONE (EXCLUDING ENDOWMENT): INSTITUTIONS GROUPED BY RELIGIOUS ORIENTATION**

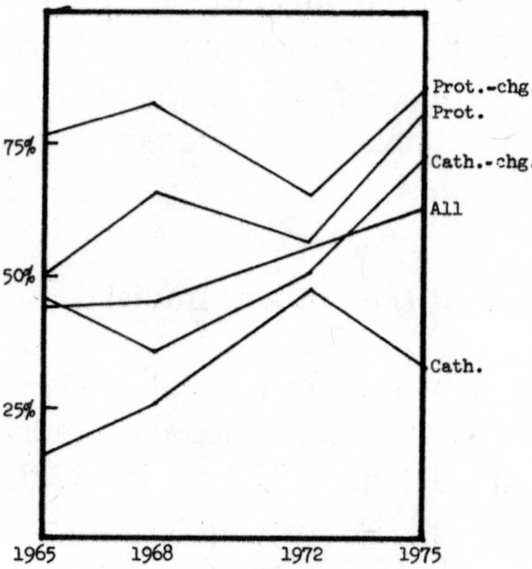

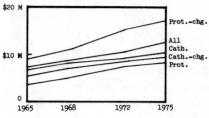

Figure 16

**DEBT/EQUITY: INSTITUTIONS GROUPED BY RELIGIOUS ORIENTATION**

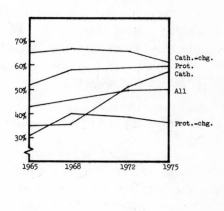

Figure 17

**TOTAL EQUITY: INSTITUTIONS GROUPED BY RELIGIOUS ORIENTATION**

Figure 18

**AVERAGE TOTAL EQUITY PER STUDENT: INSTITUTIONS GROUPED BY RELIGIOUS ORIENTATION**

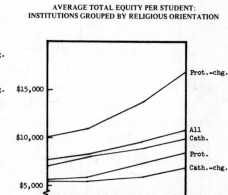

high incidence of cash-flow problems (Figure 15), average debt as a percent of equity has begun to fall (Figure 16). But equity per student (Figure 18) has declined relative to Catholic colleges and relative to all study colleges. And, of paramount importance, there has been a drop in real instructional expenditures per student (Figure 19) and a concomitant and rapid increase in student-faculty ratios (Figure 20). Because these trends are so clearly divergent from those of the other groups of colleges, it must be concluded that their educational programs have suffered to pay for the earlier growth.

### Results Grouped by Sex Composition of the Student Bodies

In contrast to the more stable growth pattern for all colleges, the mean enrollments for male-change colleges increased rapidly. Although average enrollments declined from 1972 to 1975, the average statistics are heavily influenced by two larger colleges, which coincidentally suffered from special circumstances—located in a deteriorating urban center. If median statistics are used (the dotted line on Figure 21), the trend line continues steadily upward. Although the percent of applicants accepted by these colleges rose slightly more rapidly than for all study colleges, the SAT scores are higher and declined less. During campus visits, administrators spoke glowingly of the change to coeducation. Virtually no one was dissatisfied. In sum, all the evidence suggests that the change to coeducation at these male colleges was uniformly successful in raising enrollments without lowering admission standards.

Financially, how successful was the implementation of coeducation at male colleges? Figure 28 shows that equity is growing much more rapidly at these colleges than at other colleges. But debt is rising just as rapidly, as evidenced by the debt-to-equity ratios on Figure 27. This increasing debt is paralleled by an increase in the percent of these colleges with cash flow problems (Figure 26). If endowment funds were included, however, all the colleges in this group could meet the demands of creditors.

Although under other circumstances one might take the increase in debt as a sign of weakness, it is not so in this case. The financial officers of these colleges are considerably more confident

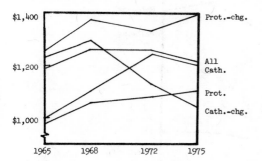

Figure 19

AVERAGE INSTRUCTIONAL EXPENDITURES PER STUDENT
(ADJUSTED FOR PRICE CHANGES):
INSTITUTIONS GROUPED BY RELIGIOUS ORIENTATION

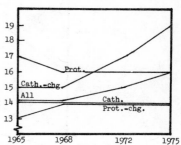

Figure 20

AVERAGE STUDENT-FACULTY RATIO:
INSTITUTIONS GROUPED BY RELIGIOUS ORIENTATION

about the finances of their colleges than were most of those with whom we spoke. This willingness to incur debt reflects, in the opinion of the author, a degree of optimism not often found on most of the other campuses.[9]

In conclusion, there are no signs that newly-adopted coeducational admissions policies have relieved these colleges of the normal financial problems facing private higher education. But enrollments have increased and administrators, including the typically doleful business manager, are optimistic. It is safe to conclude, therefore, that the policy was financially successful.

Enrollments also grew more rapidly at female-change colleges, especially when compared to female colleges. The other trends are similar to all study colleges except the average SAT scores; these have plummeted in comparison to those of female colleges, all study colleges, Catholic-change colleges, and the national average. An additional piece of information on these female-to-coeducation colleges is that the percent of commuter students rose from 51% to 71% of the total student body. No other group of institutions matched this increase.

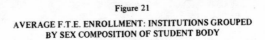

Figure 21

AVERAGE F.T.E. ENROLLMENT: INSTITUTIONS GROUPED
BY SEX COMPOSITION OF STUDENT BODY

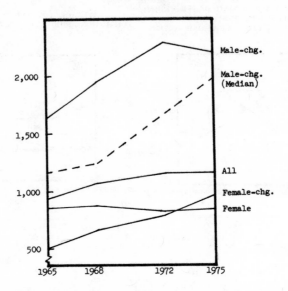

Financially, there were distinct differences between the female and female-change colleges in 1965. Figure 26 indicates that
the female colleges had decidedly fewer cash flow problems than
the female-change colleges in 1965. The female colleges also had
relatively less total debt (Figure 27) than did the female-change
colleges. Debt per student was $1,600 and $3,700 for female and
female-change colleges, respectively. Plant assets per student were
only $8,500 per student at female colleges compared to $13,000
at female-change colleges. The norm for all study colleges was
$7,000 per student in 1965. Finally, female-change colleges had a
much lower student-faculty ratio in 1965 (Figure 31). Thus, there
is evidence that the female-change institutions faced a variety
of serious financial problems. The policy of admitting men was
apparently made under the spectre of financial crisis.

Debt increased as enrollment grew at female-change colleges,
in a pattern reminiscent of male-change institutions. Since 1968,
the average debt to equity ratio for these colleges has declined to a
more moderate level. After examining all the financial data, however, prospects cannot be termed favorable. For example, average

Figure 22

AVERAGE APPLICATIONS: INSTITUTIONS GROUPED
BY SEX COMPOSITION OF STUDENT BODY

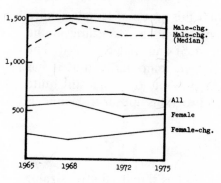

Figure 23

AVERAGE PERCENT OF APPLICANTS ACCEPTED:
INSTITUTIONS GROUPED BY SEX COMPOSITION OF
STUDENT BODY

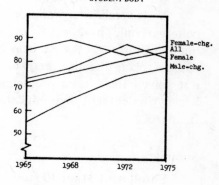

Figure 24

AVERAGE PERCENT OF STUDENTS ACCEPTED WHO
ENROLL: INSTITUTIONS GROUPED BY SEX COMPOSITION
OF STUDENT BODY

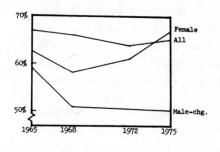

Figure 25

AVERAGE SAT SCORES: INSTITUTIONS GROUPED BY SEX
COMPOSITION OF STUDENT BODY

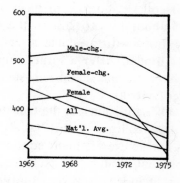

equity per student for this group shows a decidely downward slope on Figure 29; this is clearly contrary to the trend lines for other colleges. Moreover, instructional expenditures (adjusted for inflation) declined from $1,415 per student in 1965 to $1,080 per student in 1975-76 (Figure 30). The student-faculty ratios have also risen rapidly (Figure 31).

The overall interpretation is that this group of female-change colleges could have been best characterized as struggling in the middle 1960's; they were heavily in debt and underenrolled. The change to coeducation *may* have helped temporarily, but it has not solved their basic problems. At present, they are still quite heavily in debt and their educational programs appear to be under-financed.

## Summary

Enrollment at all 40 study colleges has stabilized after sizable increases in the 1960's. Data on applications, percent of students accepted, and SAT scores, however, indicate that these colleges are finding it increasingly difficult to recruit students. Adult students are becoming an ever more important component of enrollment for these colleges, confirming other published reports.

Although most of the colleges in this study are avoiding new long-term debt, cash flow problems are growing as payments on older debt increase in accord with the contractual terms and as these colleges borrow to meet summer operating needs. In June 1975 about 15% to 20% of these colleges could not meet current obligations with available assets (including most of their endowment funds). After a rather rapid rise in debt relative to equity, this statistic has stabilized—suggesting that total debt is coming under control.

Of significance is the fact that equity or net worth has grown for these colleges—and it has also increased on a per student basis. This is true even if plant equity is excluded or if institutions with enrollment declines are excluded. If an estimate for plant depreciation is included, however, equity grew only slightly.

To finance even this equity growth, colleges are increasingly reliant on outside sources of revenue, particularly the state and federal governments. Although tuition as a percent of revenue has

**Figure 26**

**PERCENT OF INSTITUTIONS WITH LIQUID RATIO LESS THAN ONE (EXCLUDING ENDOWMENT): INSTITUTIONS GROUPED BY SEX COMPOSITION OF STUDENT BODY**

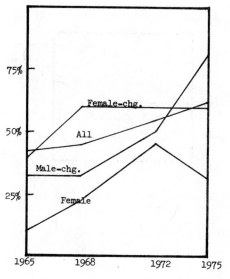

**Figure 27**

**DEBT/EQUITY: INSTITUTIONS GROUPED BY SEX COMPOSITION OF STUDENT BODY**

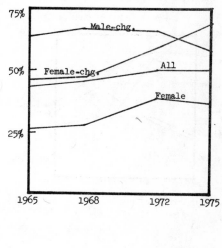

**Figure 28**

**TOTAL EQUITY: INSTITUTIONS GROUPED BY SEX COMPOSITION OF STUDENT BODY**

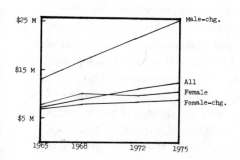

**Figure 29**

**AVERAGE TOTAL EQUITY PER STUDENT: INSTITUTIONS GROUPED BY SEX COMPOSITION OF STUDENT BODY**

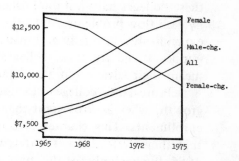

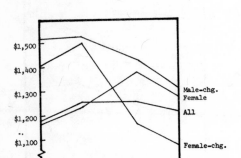

Figure 30

AVERAGE INSTRUCTIONAL EXPENDITURES PER STUDENT
(ADJUSTED FOR PRICE CHANGES): INSTITUTIONS
GROUPED BY SEX COMPOSITION OF STUDENT BODY

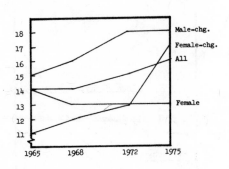

Figure 31

AVERAGE STUDENT-FACULTY RATIO: INSTITUTIONS
GROUPED BY SEX COMPOSITION OF STUDENT BODY

been stable, per student income from tuition has grown considerably more rapidly than has the consumer price index. In contrast, resources devoted to instruction have declined and the average student-faculty ratio has increased. Expenditures for administration, student aid, the library, and recruiting have risen.

In sum, the strength of these colleges appears to lie in the modest growth in equity; on average, the financial resources of these colleges have not diminished. Many are, however, threatened by cash flow problems. And although tuition is rising, instructional expenditures are falling. Finally, the government has provided important aid for these colleges. Although this support has not meant their salvation, it has certainly been an important crutch.

Protestant colleges exhibited above average enrollment growth, whereas Protestant-change colleges struggled to maintain enrollments. This chapter presents additional evidence, however, that there were distinct differences between these two groups in 1965, the beginning of the study period. Protestant-change colleges were wealthier and more selective. But since 1965, there does not appear to be any major financial advantage to a more religious or a more secular orientation at these colleges with Protestant heritages.

Catholic and Catholic-change colleges were quite similar in 1965. The major differences were that Catholic-change colleges (1) had more debt, (2) were more likely to have cash flow problems, and (3) expended more per student. It appears that, in the middle of the previous decade, the colleges that were to be labeled Catholic-change had become financially overextened: enrollment increases seemed imperative. Although more students were enrolled in Catholic-change colleges by 1975, they were considerably less bright than their predessors and the debt structure of the colleges has improved only modestly. These institutions *still* show very heavy reliance on debt. Moreover, improvements in the financial structure seem to have been achieved through severe, possibly debilitating, cuts in the instructional program.

Colleges that admitted only men and then opened their doors to women were almost uniformly successful at increasing enrollments while maintaining admission standards. Although exhibiting some absolute decline, the average SAT scores for these colleges has moved from 70 points to 80 points above the national average. Equity has also grown quite rapidly for these colleges. Their major financial blemish is their increasing by heavy debt; the author has concluded, however, that this is a result of optimism rather than necessity.

Female-change colleges also increased enrollment. For this group, however, there is strong evidence that this was accomplished by lowering admission standards. Again, the female-change colleges were heavily in debt and underenrolled at the beginning of the study period. And, like the Catholic-change colleges (of which they are a subset), they have been able to reduce their debt only by reducing instructional expenditures and raising student-faculty ratios. It appears unlikely that this policy change did much to relieve the long-run pressures that challenge these institutions.

## Chapter 5

# Summary and Conclusions

The research reported in this book compares religious colleges with religious colleges that became more secular and single-sex colleges with single-sex colleges that become coeducational. The fiscal analysis employed more than 25 indicators to determine trends in demand, liquidity, debt structure, fiscal resources, and current operations. In addition to enrollment and financial trends, the study also evaluated changes that occurred in the educational environment of the study colleges. Each of the 40 colleges was visited and key administrators were interviewed. This third stage of analysis refined the data base and added qualitative depth to the report.

Given increasingly uncertain enrollment projections, administrators in all types of American colleges and universities are considering altering their colleges' missions to expand applicant pools and thus to fill dormitories and classrooms. The findings of this study have relevance for those decisions. The first section of this concluding chapter summarizes the research findings. The final sections review their implications for college administrators and government leaders.

## Summary

### All Study Colleges

One is struck by the particularly distinctive environment of the 40 study colleges in the middle 1960's. They were typically cohesive, had high group spirit, and exhibited an obvious sense of decorum. Although not unusually scholarly, they were oriented toward instruction and were apparantly successful in this effort. One could apply this same description today but with less emphasis. That is, as a group these colleges have CUES profiles that are somewhat less distinctive. The most significant change occurred on the Propriety scale. The decline of ten percentile points indicates less emphais on manners and decorum today. Although the Community score declined only modestly (six percentile points), the drop has special importance. This is because a major competitive strength of these institutions is their "personal" environment. Administrators, however, have placed more emphasis, with mixed success, on the academic environment. Although CUES Scholarship and Quality of Teaching scale scores have risen, instructional expenditures and SAT scores are down. Confirming current reports on American higher education, students at these small private institutions appear to have turned from political concerns toward more personal, poetic, and artistic interests.

Enrollments at these colleges grew in the 1960's but have since stabilized. Information gathered on applications, acceptance rates, and SAT scores, however, suggests that these colleges are experiencing considerable difficulty in maintaining their enrollment levels. For example, Scholastic Aptitude scores are falling more rapidly at these colleges than the national average, and the percent of applicants accepted has risen rapidly.

Financially, these institutions exhibit both strengths and weaknesses. In spite of a number of lean years, they managed to modestly increase financial resources. Depending upon the assumptions used, the rate of increase is estimated to be between 1% and 6% annually. Although the estimate of 1% is probably the most realistic, it is reassuring that resources do not evidence a decline. In addition, debt has stabilized—although it has changed form. Short-term borrowing has begun to replace longer-term mortages and bonds. This reflects an acceptance of "no growth" and augurs increasing cash flow problems. In June 1975, between 15% and 20% of these colleges could not meet current debt obligations with available assets. This cash problem, aggravated by growing payments on previous debt, looms ominously in the future for them.

As operating income is squeezed, administrators at these institutions tend to pare the instructional budget. This is evidenced by the 4% decline in instructional expenditures per student since 1972. Obviously there is a limit as to how deep the budgetary knife can go before seriously affecting educational effectiveness. There has already been a noticeable increase in the average student-faculty ratio. In addition, maintenance as a percent of plant investment continues to decline as more resources are being directed toward student financial assistance, administration, and recruiting. Major relief has come to these colleges in the form of state and federal monies.

Although there are signs of environmental and financial strain, the immediate survival of most of these colleges is not threatened. These colleges were not chosen as a representative sample of private higher education, however. They were selected to represent particular subsets of private higher education. This selection afforded a comparison between private colleges that made major strategic policy changes and private colleges that were more constant with regard to their institutional missions. The results of these comparisons are viewed in the following sections.

## Protestant and Protestant-Change Colleges

Seven colleges in the study are designated as Protestant colleges. On the index of religiosity constructed for this study, these colleges were consistently at the top. Although they are not necessarily "evangelical," there is an unmistakable religious enthusiasm on campus. The religious mission of these colleges is shared by administrators and students alike. At one college, students complained that the administration was not as effective as it could be in projecting the religious atmosphere of the college to prospective students. Another college routinely included doctrinal religious questions when interviewing student applicants. Faculty were selected and evaluated on moral and religious criteria as well as on academic ones. Not surprisingly, the environment of these colleges was, and remains, distinct. Compared with the other 33 colleges in the study, the median CUES profile for these colleges has been very stable. They retain high scores in Community, Propriety, Campus Morale, and Quality of Teaching.

Enrollment growth slightly exceeded that of the other study colleges. Although SAT scores have declined somewhat more than average, campus officials are generally more confident about the future. This is because these institutions use admissions criteria other than scholastic apptitude and, by their standards, demand is strong.

Financially, the seven Protestant colleges have fared a little better than average. Total resources continue to grow without the instructional cuts common to other colleges. And although resources per student remains lower than the average for other colleges, the gap continues to narrow.

Colleges designated Protestant-change were considerably more diverse than the Protestant colleges. With respect to religious orientation, there is strong evidence that these six colleges had already changed considerably prior to the middle 1960's. In general, they had higher admission standards in 1965 and expended more per student than other colleges in the study. It is unlikely that these colleges consciously secularized; rather they seem to have responded to the wave of new students in the 1950's and 1960's and to the availability of public support. With varying success, they sought increased academic acclaim. Timing, administrative prowess, and fortune in all likelihood separate those that were successful from those that were not.

Using CUES as a measure of distinctiveness, these colleges were less unique than all study colleges in the 1960's. Their profile was much closer to the national norms. Since 1965, the profile for this group has moved even closer to the national norms. Part of this change is attributable to increases on the Scholarship and Awareness scales.

These colleges have not shown the enrollment stability of the other sub-groups since 1972. Average enrollment has declined slightly. In spite of the fact that these colleges remain wealthier than average, however, their administrators are more concerned about the future. The reason seems to be that these colleges compete more directly with the less expensive public institutions for a similar applicant pool.

## Catholic and Catholic-Change Colleges

Twelve colleges were designated as Catholic and eleven as Catholic-change. The distinction between these two sub-groups is somewhat blurred. In the 1960's, the colleges in both sub-groups tended to occupy a position between the Protestant and Protestant-change colleges on the religiosity index; moreover, all the colleges with a Catholic heritage declined on this index. Some Catholic-heritage colleges, however, resisted the changes to a greater extent than others.

In the 1960's, both of these sub-groups exhibited similar environments—decorous, personal, community and student oriented, with high morale. By 1975-76, the colleges designated Catholic had changed in ways that were similar to all study-colleges. These colleges were somewhat less well-mannered (in the conventional sense) and there was slightly less community orientation. On the other hand, morale remained high and scores for academic orientation and teaching rose.

The profile deviations at the Catholic-change colleges were far more pronounced. Declines on the propriety, community and campus morale scores were several times greater than those of the Catholic colleges. Indeed, vis-à-vis the national norms for Community and Campus Morale, the Catholic-change colleges must now be classified as only "average." Furthermore, in contrast to the Catholic colleges, these institutions showed no gains in the areas of scholarship and teaching.

In spite of the disparate environmental changes between the two subgroups, they cannot be attributed solely to the divergent religious environments. The financial data provided an alternative explanation. Although Catholic and Catholic-change colleges displayed a great deal of financial similarity in 1965, there were striking exceptions. For example, the Catholic-change colleges had $2,000 of debt per student compared to $1,200 at Catholic colleges. Similarly, debt as a percent of equity was twice as high at Catholic-change colleges. Analysis of these data suggests that, in the early 1960's the colleges that would subsequently be labeled Catholic-change undertook an expansion and financed the growth with debt. As the decade passed, enrollment did not increase as expected, and these colleges broadened their missions with the hope of attracting more students. Subsequently, enrollment did grow more rapidly at the Catholic-change colleges but, at the same time, administrators were forced to effect a number of cost savings. Consequently, the instructional expenditures per student fell 20% and the student-faculty ration rose from 15:1 to 19:1.

Although the antidotes that followed the financial exigencies undoubtedly affected the environment, the true cause is judged to be a synergistic combination of both financial and social factors. Regardless of the reason, the evidence presented here indicates that: (1) Catholic-heritage colleges with greater financial problems were more likely to deemphasize their Catholic mission; (2) enrollment at these colleges did increase more rapidly; and (3) simultaneously, the quality of the campus environment (as measured by CUES) declined significantly.

As at Protestant-change colleges, it is clear that most administrators at these Catholic-change colleges did not purposefully plan secularization. Rather, they responded to social and economic pressures in ways they thought best for their colleges. Although their decisions were different in degree from those made by administrators at "Catholic" colleges, they were similar in kind. Within the limits of the data collected for this study, it appears that those colleges that retained a more Catholic orientation exhibit greater competitive strength today.

## Female and Female-Change Colleges

As discussion proceeds from the religious/secular to the single-sex coeducation dimension, it is appropriate to begin with female and female-change colleges because so many of these institutions come from a Catholic heritage. In fact, each of the five female-change colleges is within the Catholic-change category. Therefore, discussion must be considered in that context. The financial and environmental trends at female-change colleges paralleled the trends at Catholic-change colleges. But they were always magnified—suggesting a similar but supplemental effect of coeducation.

Comparing the 1960's environment of what were to become female-change colleges to the 1960's environment of female colleges, one observes marked similarity. Both had parallel but slightly more exaggerated CUES profiles than did all study colleges. On the measures of community spirit and campus decorum, both female and female-change colleges were among the most distinct in the nation. Morale was also high for both groups and each emphasized instruction.

In spite of a few modest differences in their profile, the same description would apply today to the female colleges. The profile for the female colleges that pursued coeducation, however, changed dramatically. The median CUES scores of these colleges, with two scores excepted,[1] are now at or below national norms.

Once again, the financial data provide an additional explanation for the environmental changes. These female-change colleges, like the Catholic-change colleges, were in financial difficulty in 1965. With high investment in plant ($13,000 per student vs. $8,500 per student at female colleges), these institutions were heavily in debt and underenrolled. They needed new students.

Males now account for 28% of their student body. These men are generally local residents who chose the college because it was convenient; most have considerably less academic ability than the women. Although debt has declined, total resources per student have also fallen. That is, these colleges have fewer financial resources with which to support the education of their students. Concomitantly, instructional expenditures per student have been cut by more than 20% and the student-faculty ratio has risen from 11:1 to 17:1.[2] In addition, the change to coeducation has not especially pleased the female students. Students at female-change colleges were almost twice as likely as students at female colleges to select "social life" as the least attractive characteristic of their colleges (30% vs. 16%).

Although the administrators at some of these colleges may have had few alternatives to coeducation, some already regret the change. As one president asserted: "Had we recognized the incipient feminist movement, we would not have attempted coeducation at [this college]."

## Male-Change Colleges

Lest some readers conclude that change is inadvisable, this

section closes with a discussion of male-change colleges. The comments of one dean perhaps best capsulize the findings: "Being the resident crank around here for 26 years, there were few policies with which I couldn't find fault. But I must admit that the admission of women to [this college] was an unqualified success. Everyone, with the possible exception of athletic coaches, is pleased."

Indeed, enrollment growth at male-change colleges exceeded the trends at other study colleges. SAT scores were more stable because the women were at least equal to the men in academic study and often superior. As evidenced by CUES profiles, the changes were environmentally successful. When queried about alumni support, most college officials responded that it had fallen only slightly because the alumni had been kept well informed. Although some graduates regretted the move to coeducation, they understood the potential advantages. Gifts from alumni showed only the slightest drop in the first year following the change. The only unexpected wrinkle was Title IX of the Education Amendments of 1972. Some colleges have reported unexpected expansion of their athletic facilities to accommodate women. But this is a minor consideration when evaluating the success of coeducation at male colleges.

Unfortunately, it has been the very success of male colleges' adoption of coeducation that has exacerbated the problems at women's colleges. In one instance it was specifically the admission of women at a "brother school" that prompted administrators at a female college to announce a coeducational admissions policy.

## Tasks for Administration

In the 1960's, the college-age population was expanding and the percent of young adults attending college was increasing. If the dormitories weren't filled this year, they would be next year. Colleges grew almost without regard to their mission or the effectiveness of their management. Those times have passed and a new era of stabilization and retrenchment has arrived. Now, more than ever, college administrators must effectively manage their college's resources—educational as well as financial.

Fiscal Management

Another full litany of suggestion for effective management would serve little purpose here. A few points warrant special attention, however. When managing fiscal resources, the first problem administrators must confront is measurement. This report has reviewed some of the criticisms of college and university financial reporting. The new guidelines published by the American Institute of Certified Public Accountants are very helpful in making the financial reports more uniform. This format, however, is intended for reporting to the public. College administrators must give high priority to internal financial information systems. Several methods and measures of this report were helpful to the researchers. Generally the aggregation of fund data and the use of ratios seem to be efficient and reasonable approaches. Specifically, measures of total equity and liquidity indicators are quite useful. It is recommended, however, that each college organize an *internal* financial reporting format specific to its own situation. This may include more than just special measures. Many commerical enterprises regularly prepare several sets of financial records. Some records follow tax regulations and/or accounting guidelines so that the firm will remain within reporting regulations and pay legally minimum tax. Other records are based on the most realistic cost information that their accountants can provide and are used by management for financial evaluation and planning. Realistic and comprehensive financial information is particularly important for colleges today. For example, almost all colleges in this study were expanding or planning to expand their adult education programs. Prices are being set, however, on the basis of guesswork and hunches. Additionally, colleges may wish to follow the lead of the University of Rochester and categorize funds as expendable and nonexpendable. Such a division would be particularly useful in evaluating cash flow—an area of increasing concern.

Average income per insitution at the study colleges was about $4.5 million in 1974-75. Yet the financial staffs typically consisted of one professional and a few clerk-assistants. At a few institutions, almost all decisions on financial data collection and reporting are made by outside auditors who visit the college once a year. Administrators cannot expect better financial information unless they are willing to commit resources to the endeavor.

Another problem is neglect of information that is available. Business officers commonly complained that, when they prepared reports, academic administrators would not take the time and trouble to understand them. Seminars on financial reporting and decision-making would help. But the real issue concerns the integration of academic and financial decision-making.

## Educational Resource Management

Faced with reduced demand, college administrators have two basic alternatives. They can pursue the same mission with increased effectiveness or they can change their mission with the hope of widening their applicant pool. (Although this dichotomy oversimplifies the strategic decisions confronted by college officials, it is fundamentally accurate.) This study suggests that, *although the pursuit of an expanded mission may have immediate financial advantages, there are often long-term competitive disadvantages.* Enrollment tended to increase more rapidly at the colleges in this study that broadened their educational mission, but many of these "change" colleges lost much of their special environmental character. Because these colleges must charge relatively high tuition, *the loss of their unique characteristics is likely to make recruiting students in the future especially difficult. Similar to colleges that supplement their budgets by using endowment principal, these "change" colleges may be considered to have expended educational capital*, a resource that is even more difficult to replace. Obviously, such a policy offers only short-term advantages and may be disastrous in the long-run.

Although the problems are real, they should not be construed as hopeless. College officials are aware of the need to offer an attractive product—witness the number of colleges that have embraced career education or life-long learning or values education. But it is precisely this herd-like reflex that mitigates against a truly successful and competitive policy. So many colleges seem to be "independently" pursuing the same educational innovations—most of them launched at last year's A.A.H.E. meeting. The successful administrators will be those who chart a different course or even dare to sail against the current. For some colleges, it may mean an affirmation of their traditional mission. For others it will be a special interpretation of a new trend. But because the journey must be creative, it is impossible to set the directions here. The administrators at each college must evaluate their strengths, their weaknesses, and the risks they are willing to assume.

These generalizations notwithstanding, the researchers did encounter a number of creative policies that are likely to interest administrators of other colleges. For example, one women's college implemented coeducation with relative success. By heavily supporting athletic scholarships, the college "purchased" a basketball team and catapulted itself into local athletic fame. Another college, reasserting its Catholic heritage, reoriented its nursing program to emphasize the ministerial responsibilities of Catholic nurses. Another women's college has combined its single-sex feminist orientation with career education, including internships in accounting, marketing, and public administration. This program has proved to be very attractive to career-oriented young women.

When trying to preserve educational resources, administrators will find measures like the College and University Environmental Scales particularly useful. Quantitative measures are important because they provide a summary standard of comparison. Although a few numbers cannot capture the limitless dimensions of complex organizations, they are a convenient starting point. Used as trouble signals, they can trigger a more thorough investigation. Without standard quantitative measures, it is too easy to relegate concerns about educational resources to the annual convocation. After these autumn remarks, administrative time then becomes fully consumed by more immediate and measureable concerns—budgets, contracts, and enrollments.

### Tasks for Public Officials

Many reports have reviewed the financial condition of private higher education; the conclusions have been mixed. The findings of Bowen and Minter, for example, tended to be positive.[3] The conclusions of Lanier and Andersen, covering approximately the same time period (early 1970's), are more pessimistic.[4] This report reviews a longer time span and offers a financial assessment that supports aspects of both reports. The colleges in this study have managed to build financial equity since 1965, but they are now beset by cash flow problems, and there are general declines in real instructional expenditures. Maintenance is suffering, and the financial independence of these colleges is less secure. There are considerations other than the strictly financial ones however. Bowen and Minter conclude their report by questioning whether private colleges may be losing the very distinctiveness that makes their survival important.[5] This question was a focal point of this research.

In the introduction, it was suggested that, although the decline in the number of single-sex and religious colleges may be unfortunate simply because public institutions cannot assume these missions, there was an additional consideration. That is, if these colleges are losing a special and distinctive educational environment as they seek new students, then the trends are of more concern. Indeed, unwelcome environmental changes are more likely to have occurred at colleges that broadened their mission than at the more constant institutions. Many of these study colleges scored in the highest percentiles on the community, campus morale, and quality of teaching and student-faculty relationship scales of CUES in the 1960's. The attributes these scales are intended to measure are those that Astin and Lee find especially conducive to student development.[6] Yet those colleges that have become coeducational or significantly more secular now rank very near the national average on these scales.

Regrettable as these changes may be, public action is still unjustified unless it is likely to provide relief. Perhaps these "change" colleges responded to social trends—trends that would probably prove impervious to public policy. Undeniably, there is some truth in such an assertion. It is impossible to determine the impact of broader social trends, however, because of the way higher education is financed in this country. Special purpose private colleges are not, and were not, competing solely on their educational merits. Many students who might attend religious, single-sex, or other special purpose private institutions are undoubtedly dissuaded by the additional cost of attending these colleges. Thus, the problem for private colleges is to find enough relatively affluent students who are willing to pay their tuition charges. *As more private colleges seek to expand their applicant pool by broadening their missions (single-sex to coeducation, religiously oriented to secular education, the inclusion of career education with liberal arts, an education for the academically disinclined as well as the gifted, and an education for the mature adult as well as the young adult), one can anticipate a further demise of diversity with a concomitant erosion of distinctive educational environments.*

Paradoxically, as private institutions become less distinct, students will be even less likely to pay their higher tuition charges. This is not a problem that administrators of private colleges can resolve. It is a problem for public officials and the electorate.

## Tuition Gap

This report will not review the numerous proposals for aiding private institutions. Excellent summaries have recently been published by the National Council of Independent Colleges and Universities.[7] One point deserves emphasis, however. If private special purpose colleges are to compete effectively, aid to students cannot be based solely on student need. Need-based aid is, of course, necessary and important. But it does not serve the central constituency of these colleges—the middle class. As long as the additional cost of attending a private special purpose college is two or three thousand dollars a year, middle-class students will drift toward public institutions. Admittedly, significant aid to middle-class students would be expensive. Nor should it be financed by reducing aid to low-income students. But assisting middle-class students at private colleges may reduce public burden in the long-run. In the absence of significant aid, the relative burden of financing higher education will continue to shift to the states because of increased enrollments at public institutions. For example in 1965 the share of total public and private educational and general income contributed by the states was 29%. Seven years later, in 1972-73, the share had risen to 36%. The absolute increase was $5 billion dollars.[8] It seems that the states can hardly afford to withold assistance to parents who send their children to private colleges. *Put simply, to maintain diversity and to limit public expenditures, tuition assistance must be offered to the middle-income family.*

The federal government has done very little to aid middle-income students beyond increasing their access to credit. The most popular prospect for increasing federal assistance appears to be tax relief. To date, none of the tax relief proposals has survived the legislative process. The chief reason seems to be the fear of lost tax revenues.[9] If tax relief were specifically *targeted at families with students in private colleges (e.g., tax credits based on costs over $2,000), the revenue loss would be much less, however.* The reason for this savings is, of course, that 80% of students are now enrolled in public colleges and universities. But it is this very fact that erodes the political attractiveness of such a plan. If we are to preserve other than the ordinary educational choices, some extraordinary political leadership may be called for.

Reducing the tuition gap is a long-range solution. Even if support could be mobilized, it would take time to implement and additional years for competitive stability to be achieved. There are other measures that state and federal governments can take.

## Federal Loans

The federal government encouraged private institutions to expand in the 1960's by financing the expansion of their facilities. As generous as the terms of these loans are, administrators at many of these colleges find they are under severe pressure to maintain enrollments or use their facilities in some other way. For example, one Catholic college in the study had become considerably more dependent on commuter and part-time students. Thus it became impossible for the institution to fill both its dormitores, one of which was federally financed. In the face of a persistent debt obligation, college officials leased one dormitory to the state to be used as an extension of the state police academy. Although this arrangement served as a financial palliative, the potential environmental consequences are obvious. To reduce the necessity for this type of action, *the federal government should review the impact of debt repayment at private colleges and consider possible refinancing arrangements.*

## State and Federal Regulations

Although this study has no quantitative measure of the burden of state and federal regulation, it was a commonly expressed concern of college officials. They mention the not insignificant clerical burden. But more worrisome to these officials is the prospect of and actual intrusion by government into college policy decisions. For example, when seeking a new president, the trustees of one religious college attempted to restrict the search to church members. The state Equal Opportunity Commission prohibited such a restriction, however. Clearly this type of interference threatens the independence, and therefore the diversity, of American colleges and universities.

## Cash Flow

The federal and state governments have typically acted on a case-by-case basis to assist private colleges with special financial problems. The evidence in this report suggests that there is an increasing number of colleges with cash flow problems—that is, colleges that cannot meet summer payroll without incurring dangerously high short-term debt. Assisting these colleges in a case-by-case fashion will be too cumbersome. The danger is that, once the problem becomes publically recognized, students may be reluctant to enroll and creditors may demand payment. *It is therefore recommended that the federal or state governments establish a "public line of credit" for private colleges.* This would reduce the risk of a minor cash problem snowballing into a major institutional catastrophe before any government agency can assist. Obviously more debt is not a long-term solution for these colleges. But until a system of permanent relief can be arranged, immediate access to credit may save a number of small and inadequately endowed private colleges.

## Concluding Remarks

This research effort is not intended to justify any particular educational orientation. I do not advocate religious education or single-sex education. Nor do I favor coeducation or a secular orientation in higher education. Leaders at each college must set the goals for their institutions based upon commonly shared values and a realistic assessment of societal trends and forces. The intention of this research was to expand the dimensions of policy discussion. Too few policy analysis bridge educational and financial concerns. It is clear, however, that financial and educational decisions are inextricably entwined. Analyses at both the institutinal and the national level must recognize this. By merely counting students or summing dollars, we run the risk of allowing valuable educational resources to erode.

Diversity has been a hallmark in American higher education for many years. Enrollment of traditional students is now ebbing. As it does, many colleges are scrambling for new students and expanding their missions. It is, however, very difficult for an institution to narrow its mission and recapture its distinctive environment after expansion. It is important, therefore, that every effort be made to maintain diversity in this current period, which is optimistically labeled "steady state."

# Notes

**Chapter 1**

1 George Stigler, *The Theory of Price* (New York: Macmillan, 1967); also see Robert Dorfman, *Prices and Markets* (Englewood Cliffs: Prentice-Hall, 1967).
2 Although there are a few publicly-supported single-sex, undergraduate colleges remaining, Title IX of the Education Amendments of 1972 prohibits the creation of any new such institutions.
3 From a count of institutions listed in *Education Directory*, 1966-67 (Washington, D.C.: United States Government Printing Office, 1967); *Higher Education Directory*, 1973-74 (Washington, D.C. United States Government Printing Office, 1975). Talmudical institutions and service academies were not counted.
4 *Ibid.*
5 Although students always cite educational criteria as their main reasons for selecting a college, it has been found that the variable that is most closely correlated (negatively) with changing preferences is price. See Richard E. Anderson, "Determinants of Institutional Attractiveness to Bright, Prospective College Students," *Research in Higher Education* IV, 4, 1976.
6 Howard Bowen and W. John Minter, *Private Higher Education* (Washington, D.C.: Association of American Colleges, 1975), p. 79.

**Chapter 2**

1 Manning M. Pattillo, Jr., and Donald M. Mackenzie, *Church-Sponsored Higher Education in the United States* (Washington, D.C.: American Council on Education, 1966).
2 Andrew M. Greeley, William C. McCready, and Kathleen McCourt, *Catholic Schools in a Declining Church* (Kansas City: Sheed and Ward, 1976).
3 Because the CUES scoring procedures have changed, the earlier results were rescored as directed in the *CUES: Second Edition Technical Manual*. For two administrations in the

1960's and for five in the 1975-76, there were fewer respondents than the recommended minimum. This is not a serious problem, however, because the results for any one institution are grouped with those of other institutions.

4    The second edition has 160 items. The last 60 questions have no counterpart in the first edition; This is not a problem, however, because they are not used to create the scale scores.

5    The base score for each of the first five scales is 20. Because 20 items create these scales, the scores range from 0 to 40. The Campus Morale subscale has 22 items and a base score of 22. The Quality of Teaching subscale has 11 items and a base score of 11. Hence, the scores on these two scales range from 0 to 44 and from 0 to 22, respectively.

6    C. Robert Pace, *College and University Environmental Scales: Second Edition Technical Manual* (Princeton: Educational Testing Service, 1969), p. 11.

7    *Ibid.*, p. 45.

8    *Ibid.*, p. 54.

9    Douglas J. Collier, *The Determination of Institutional Financial Distress: A Proposal for Decision Making,* preliminary draft (Boulder: National Center for Higher Education Management Systems, 1973); Maryanne Carroll, *An Adoption of Financial Analysis to Higher Education* (Boulder: National Center for Higher Education Management Systems, 1973); Douglas J. Collier, *A Discussion of Institutional Financial Analysis* (Boulder: National Center for Higher Education Management Systems, 1973); Douglas J. Collier, *The Analysis of Institutional Financial Health: A Workshop Report* (Boulder: National Center for Higher Education Management Systems, 1973).

10    Howard R. Bowen and W. John Minter, *Private Higher Education* (Washington, D.C.: Association of American Colleges, 1975). See also 1976 and 1977 editions.

11    Lyle H. Lanier and Charles J. Anderson, *A Study of the Financial Condition of Colleges and Universities: 1972-1975* (Washington, D.C.: American Council on Education, 1975).

12    D. Kent Halstead, *Higher Education Prices and Price Indexes* (Washington, D.C.: U.S. Government Printing Office, 1975), and 1976 Supplement.

13    Richard G. Wynn, "Inflation Indicators in Liberal Arts Colleges" (unpublished Ph.D. dissertation, University of Michigan, 1974).

14    Hans H. Jenny, *The Consolidated Net Worth of Private Colleges* (Wooster, Ohio: The College of Wooster, 1973).

15    C.W. Bastable, "Collegiate Accounting Needs Re-Evaluation," *The Journal of Accounting* (December 1973).

16    Price, Waterhouse, and Company, *Position Paper on College and University Reporting* (New York: Price, Waterhouse, 1975).

17    William M. Wilkinson, "The Fiction of 'Restricted' Funds in Institutional Accounting," *College and University Business Officer*, Vol. X, No. 3 (September 1976).

18    Benjamin Graham, David L. Dodd, and Sidney Cottle, *Security Analysis* (New York: McGraw-Hill, 1962); see also Harry G. Gutham, *Analysis of Financial Statements* (Englewood Cliffs: Prentice-Hall, 1953); and Douglas A. Hayes, *Investments: Analysis and Management* (New York: Macmillan, 1961).

19    "Ten Eastern Colleges Accused of Crying Wolf in Reporting Deficits," *Wall Street Journal*, April 27, 1973.

20    This assertion is made within the context of currently standard reporting practices. Wilkinson of the University of Rochester recommends categorizing funds as expendable and non-expandable and listing unexpended restricted fund balances as deferred revenues (see note 17). His recommendations make sense. If they were widely accepted, the distinction between restricted and unrestricted funds for the purpose of *balance sheet analysis* would be moot.

21    For a more thorough discussion of price indicies, see Halstead, *Higher Education Prices*, and Lanier and Anderson, *Study of the Financial Condition*, Chapter VI.

## Chapter 3

1    Alexander W. Astin and Calvin B.T. Lee, *The Indivisible Colleges, A Profile of Small, Private Colleges with Limited Resources* (New York: The Carnegie Commision on Higher Education/McGraw-Hill, 1972), pp. 99, excerpted from Carol Hemstadt

Shulman, "Private Colleges: Present Conditions and Future Prospects" (Washington, D.C.: American Association of Higher Education, 1974), p. 22.

2 The problem only pertains to this stage of analysis. Later, when examining subgroups, the trend for the 40 colleges is used as a standard.

3 See also C. Robert Pace, *Education and Evangelism* (New York: The Carnegie Commission on Higher Education/McGraw-Hill, 1972), p. 96.

4 C. Robert Pace, *CUES: Second Edition Technical Manual* (Princeton: Educational Testing Service, 1969), p. 10.

## Chapter 4

1 During the course of campus interviews, the researchers uncovered evidence that the decline in test scores may be more pronounced than has been reported by most institutions. In recent years, many of these study colleges began admitting "special students" for whom test scores are either not required or not reported. One admissions officer candidly explained that the test scores for these students are not included in reports of test scores because of concern about institutional image and because of anticipated resistance from faculty over admitting "special students." Because these students were less common in the 1960's, there appears to be a systematic bias in the trend data.

2 Tabulation provided by Educational Testing Service in private correspondence, May 20, 1976.

3 In notation form,

$$\frac{\Sigma\,(a_i)}{\Sigma\,(b_i)} \neq \Sigma\left(\frac{(a_i)}{(b_i)}\right)$$

4 American Institute of Certified Public Accountants, *Audits of Colleges and Universities* (New York: AICPA, 1973), p. 21.

5 Carnegie Commission on Higher Education, *The More Effective Use of Resource* (New York: McGraw-Hill, 1972), p. 65.

6 *Ibid.*, p. 17.

7 The price index used here was the one developed by Richard Wynn specifically for instructional expenditures at liberal arts

colleges. Halstead's index was not used here because of the problem in disaggregating it for the separate components of the educational and general category. Had it been used, the trend would have been: $1,185; $1,256; $1,257; and $1,215. For all other categories, Halstead's index was used.

8 Another problem with these data is that maintenance expenditures for auxiliary operations are included in the aggregate category "auxiliary expenditures." There was no convenient way to estimate the size of these expenditures. The ratio therefore understates the true costs of maintenance. If longitudinal bias exists in the ratios, however, it is likely to be slight.

9 This debt was used to finance the planned expansion of dormitories and other general plants. But for at least two colleges in this group according to campus officials, the provisions of Title IX of the Education Amendments of 1972 necessitated an unplanned expansion of athletic facilities for women.

## Chapter 5

1 The exceptions are the Propriety and Quality of Teaching scales. Both declined noticeably but remain near the 70th percentile when ranked against national norms.

2 This is probably not an unreasonable ratio, but the instructional expenditures are low.

3 Howard R. Bowen and W. John Minter, *Private Higher Education* (Washington, D.C.: Association of American Colleges, 1975).

4 Lyle H. Lanier and Charles J. Andersen, *A Study of the Financial Condition of Colleges and Universities: 1972-1975* (Washington, D.C.: American Council on Education, 1975).

5 Bowen and Minter, *Private Higher Education*, p. 79.

6 Alexander Astin and Calvin B.T. Lee, *The Invisible Colleges: A Profile of Small, Private Colleges with Limited Resources* (New York: The Carnegie Commission on Higher Education/McGraw-Hill, 1972), p. 99.

7 Task Force of the National Council of Independent Colleges and Universities, *A National Policy for Private Higher Education* (Washington, D.C.: American Association of Higher Education,

1974; William H. McFarlane, A. E. Dick Howard, and Joy L. Chronister, *State Financial Measures Involving the Private Sector of Higher Education* (Washington, D.C.: American Association of Higher Education, 1974).

8 *Digest of Educational Statistics: 1975 Edition* (Washington, D.C.: United States Government Printing Office, 1976), Table 118.

9 Larry L. Leslie, *Higher Education Tax Allowances: An Analysis* (University Park, Pa.: Center for the Study of Higher Education, Pennsylvania State University, 1976).

MICHIGAN CHRISTIAN COLLEGE LIBRARY
ROCHESTER, MICHIGAN